PROPHET OF LOVE

Understanding the Book of Hosea

William J. Doorly

PAULIST PRESS
New York/Mahwah, N.J.

Excerpts from *Composition and Tradition in the Book of Hosea* by Gale Yee is reprinted with the permission of the author and the publisher, Scholars Press. The Bible text is from the *Revised Standard Version Bible,* copyright 1946, 1952, 1971 by the Division of Christian Education of the National Council of the Churches of Christ in the USA, and is used with permission.

Library of Congress Cataloging-in-Publication Data

Doorly, William J., 1913–
    Prophet of love: understanding the book of Hosea/William J. Doorly.
        p. cm.
    Includes bibliographical references.
    ISBN 0-8091-3241-9
    1. Bible. O.T. Hosea—Criticism, interpretation, etc.   2. Bible. O.T.
Hosea—Theology.   I. Title.
BS1565.2.D66   1991
224'.6066—dc20   91-10536
                                                                                    CIP

Published by Paulist Press
997 Macarthur Boulevard
Mahwah, New Jersey 07430

Printed and bound in the
United States of America

Contents

This book is dedicated to my mother,
Marion (Edmondson) Doorly,
with thanks for her constant love and encouragement.

Introduction

Although Hosea is a profound book with gripping images ranging from tender to violent, the book shares characteristics with other prophetic books which present problems for the modern reader and the Bible student. These problems include unexpected shifts in mood, abrupt changes of direction, references to obscure (to us) geographical names, and forms of speech more at home in an ancient culture completely alien to our own. For the modern reader to understand and appreciate the eighth century prophets some preparation is needed. What is helpful first is to set aside modern expectations concerning what a book is and how a book should be written. Second, after setting aside these subjective, conditioned expectations, which take the form of pre-judgments, it is necessary to have some understanding of the time and place of origin, ancient Israel. Third, the reader must understand that these books reached their final form as the result of the contribution of several authors involving several distinct but identifiable stages.

A word about cultural distance in Hosea is needed. In dealing with Hosea the cultural distance is even more exotic than that of other biblical books. The Bible as we have it is the product of Judah, the southern kingdom of ancient Israel. As we spend time reading the books of the Bible and studying them, we begin to feel more comfortable with the culture which produced them, that is, the culture of the southern kingdom, Judah. When we turn to parts of the book of Hosea, however, we are taking a step beyond Judah, into the culture of the northern kingdom of Israel. These two ancient cultures were not identical. Even in ancient times the two kingdoms did not merge successfully with the exception of the eleventh century.

While there is nothing we can do (or should do) to make the prophetic books flow smoothly for the modern student, there are ways of approaching these books which enable us to unlock many of their mysteries. And there is a deep feeling of satisfaction which comes when a student begins to understand how the pieces of the puzzle fit together to display an intriguing picture of the book's development and the messages of the book's authors and scribal editors.

The purpose of this book is to make Hosea easier to understand and to assist the reader in appreciating important recent scholarship concerning the development of this unique prophetic work.

PART ONE

PART ONE

CHAPTER I

The Historical Hosea

Hosea, son of Beeri, is one of the four eighth century prophets whose oracles form the basis of books in the Hebrew Bible. The other three are Amos of Tekoa, Micah of Moresheth, and Isaiah of Jerusalem. These eighth century prophets are the first biblical characters without a veil of myth and legend. This does not mean that the historical outlines of these prophets are sharp. On the contrary, we have very few hard facts to assist us in our effort to picture them as distinct individuals.

Hosea, Amos, Isaiah, and Micah perform no miracles, and, apart from some Isaiah narrative, do not play a key role in the nation's history. They are not presented as deliverers of the people, nor are they pictured as being in positions of great importance in the nation's history. Their place in the history of Israel—and they occupy an important, strategic position—is determined by the words which they spoke and the ideas which they presented in their oracles—in other words, their preaching.

There are two "histories" covering these times (eighth century) in the Bible. The first is the Deuteronomistic History written in several stages beginning in the reign of Josiah (640–609) and continuing into the exile. This Deuteronomistic History constitutes the books of Joshua, Judges, Samuel and Kings. The second history, written later, after the exile for the restored community of Judah, is found in Chronicles. Neither of these histories provides us with any information concerning Hosea.

The fact that there are no stories of Hosea is not entirely negative however. The Deuteronomistic History is a theological history, omitting large periods of time and large areas of important fact. It is best viewed as a "theological" history, with its particular viewpoints on prophecy and the purpose served by prophets in Israel's past. It is common for this historian to tell stories for a theological purpose, to make a point or to illustrate a Deuteronomic theological viewpoint, always for the spiritual benefit of his readers. If there were a story, or stories, of Hosea included, we could not be certain that the stories would contribute to our quest for understanding of the "historical" Hosea.

Now, although we have stated that the Deuteronomistic History is not a history in the modern sense of the word, the reader should not get the impression that this body of literature is to be treated lightly. It is a tremendous source of information for us concerning the history of Israel as seen through Judean/Deuteronomic eyes. Besides, it is one of the great examples of world literature. We are going to become more familiar with the Deuteronomistic History as we learn about the development of the book of Hosea, and the development of the Deuteronomistic History is going to help us to understand the book of Hosea.

If we are going to learn about Hosea, we are going to learn about him from his oracles and narrative material in the book of Hosea. This defines our first problem. The oracles of the eighth century prophets comprise only a portion of the final books which bear their names. For example, (in my opinion) the oracles of Amos comprise about twenty-eight percent of the book of Amos.

So while it is possible to learn much about a prophet like Hosea from his words, there are several obstacles here. We have already reported that stories of the prophets in the "history" of Israel and Judah (Deuteronomistic History) served the theological purposes and conformed to the presuppositions of the Deuteronomistic circle which produced them. It is further recognized that Deuteronomic language and expressions (of a hundred years after the eighth century when Hosea lived) can be found liberally scattered throughout the books which bear the names of the eighth century prophets. If it were possible to identify the oracles of the eighth century (eliminating all later additions to the books by editors and redactors) we would have another problem. We would have·to identify "stereotypical" phrases and expressions used by the prophets. It is possible that at least some of the language used in the oracles which the prophets delivered was "traditional" and expected. If this were true, then we would have to identify these "expected" phrases and separate them from the prophet's completely original oracles, since stereotypical phraseology would hardly reveal anything about the individual speaker. The truth is that we know relatively little about the original, oral delivery of the prophets to their audiences.

But we keep this in mind: In each prophetic book there is a core of original oracles (which were later enlarged, added to, rearranged and restructured to meet the needs of a later time). In order to determine these original oracles we have to rely on the work of biblical historians and linguistic scholars. Now I don't want to completely discourage my readers, but we have to remind ourselves of a hard fact. Linguistic scholars do not always agree on everything. There is some good news here, however. Since the experts can't ultimately solve every problem for us, we have an opportunity to use our intuitive powers and imagination. There is an exciting possibility for us to develop a hypothesis concerning which oracles are the original oracles of the prophet, and then test that hypothesis to see how the many pieces of the puzzle fit together. Some circular reasoning is involved, but let's not be fearful. We'll launch out into the deep and enjoy what may be for us a new experience. And in due respect to our linguistic scholars, we must rely heavily on their work to sharpen our intuition.

IDENTIFYING LATER ADDITIONS TO THE PROPHETIC BOOKS

In 1945 an English professor at Temple University, Walter Ferguson, wrote a beautiful book entitled *Journey Through the Bible*.[1] His chapter on Hosea is called "The Baker Takes a Wife." Dr. Ferguson identified Hosea as a baker, basing his assumption on several verses in the book, including: "They are like a heated oven, whose baker ceases to stir the fire, from the kneading of the dough until it is leavened" (7:4), and "Ephraim is a cake not turned" (7:8).

Dr. Ferguson may be or may not be correct about Hosea's occupation, but the question which has to be answered is whether the words quoted above (concerning the activity of a baker) are the words of Hosea or the words of a redactor who lived a century later. To understand the details in Hosea means that we have to understand its development. We must identify the original oracles and the social setting of these and subsequent sayings.

One way to determine the original oracles of Hosea (or Amos or Micah) is to start by eliminating oracles and other material (sentences, phrases, words) which can be identified as probable later additions. These are some of the things we can look for:

(a) Third person narratives, stories or facts about the prophet which call the prophet by name, were written by someone else. Amos did not call himself Amos and Hosea did not call himself Hosea. These sections may have been written by eyewitnesses, or by someone a hundred years later, but they were not written by the original prophet. This includes the opening verse:

> The word of the Lord that came to Hosea the son of Beeri, in the days of Uzziah, Jotham, Ahaz, and Hezekiah, kings of Judah, and in the days of Jeroboam the son of Joash, king of Israel (1:1).

(b) Some oracles can be dated by historical perspective. For example, many scholars have identified the following passage as exilic:

> For the children of Israel shall dwell many days without king or prince, without sacrifice or pillar, without ephod or teraphim. Afterward the children of Israel shall return and seek the Lord their God, and David their king, and they shall come in fear to the Lord and to his goodness in the latter days (3:4–5).

(c) Some passages are surely Deuteronomistic. They will have Deuteronomistic words and expressions and Deuteronomistic theological perspectives.

> When Israel was a child, I loved him, and out of Egypt I
>   called my son. . . .
> Yet it was I who taught Ephraim to walk,

I took them up in my arms; but they did not know that I
    healed them (11:1–3).

Compare the above thoughts with these from Deuteronomy.

And in the wilderness . . . God bore you, as a man bears
his son. Yet in spite of this work you did not believe the
Lord your God (1:31–32).

Later in this book we will give further illustrations of Deuteronomistic passages in the book of Hosea. We will be dealing
with two periods of Deuteronomistic redaction of Hosea. One we
call Josianic and the other we will call exilic.

(d) The closing paragraph is generally agreed to be an epi-
logue. It has the flavor of wisdom literature. I will call it an addition of the exilic redactor:

Whoever is wise, let him understand these things;
whoever is discerning, let him know them;
for the ways of the Lord are right,
    and the upright walk in them,
    but transgressors stumble in them (14:9).

THE MARRIAGE OF HOSEA

One thing we can be sure about Hosea is that he had a bad
marriage. Or did he? (There is at least one scholar who believed
that Gomer was completely faithful to Hosea after the wedding.[2])
We may have to look carefully at the material. The narrative
interwoven in the first three chapters of Hosea concerning his
marriage to Gomer bat Diblaim presents a few problems. At first
reading, these chapters seem to present facts about Hosea and his
marital problems caused by a poor marriage, even though it is a
little convoluted in the telling. On close examination, however,
multiple difficulties appear. Let's look at some questions which
scholars have raised concerning Hosea's marriage.

1. The wife of chapter 1 is Gomer Bat Diblaim. The adul-

teress in chapter 3 is not named. Is this another woman, and another experience of Hosea?

2. Was Gomer unfaithful after her marriage to Hosea? We note that she is called a ". . . wife of harlotry," and one of her children is called "Not My People," but there is no verse which specifically uses her name to say Gomer was unfaithful to Hosea after the marriage.

3. If Gomer was an adulteress after her marriage to Hosea, why wasn't she punished with death? According to Leviticus 20:10, "If a man commits adultery with the wife of his neighbor, both the adulterer and the adulteress shall be put to death."

4. If Gomer was divorced by Hosea, how was he able to take her back. In chapter 2 the author pictures the relationship between Israel and Yahweh as a divorce, and the woman says: "I will go and return to my first husband." Deuteronomy 24:4 forbids a husband taking a former wife who has been defiled:

> . . . then her former husband, who sent her away, may not take her again to be his wife, after she has been defiled; for it is an abomination before the Lord.

5. Chapter 3 is written in the first person.

> And the Lord said to me, "Go again, love a woman who is beloved of a paramour and is an adultress" (3:1).

The author is telling us what Yahweh instructed him to do, to love a woman who is an adulteress. Is this a retelling of the event of Chapter 1 which is written in the third person?

> When the Lord first spoke through Hosea, the Lord said to Hosea, "Go, take to yourself a wife of harlotry" (1:2).

Because of the difference in person, some scholars have seen two different authors here and have suggested that chapter 3 is parallel to chapter 1.

6. What about the children of Hosea with the names

"Jezreel," "Not Pitied," and "Not My People"? Is this an allegorical tradition or actual fact? (Isaiah is also reported to have had children with theologically and politically significant names.)

Our purpose in this chapter is not to resolve these questions. We will offer solutions later. What we are saying is that even the information about the marriage experience in the early chapters of the book may give us only ambiguous information about the historical Hosea.

THE SEVERAL AUTHORS OF HOSEA

It is a shared belief among Bible scholars, and hardly disputed, that the book of Hosea had more than one author. Because of this the question concerning the historical Hosea is only one of many questions for which we seek answers. But there is a unique curiosity about the original prophet. Knowledge of him is a logical starting place. But by raising the questions listed above we are preparing ourselves to ask further questions, such as: Which are the *original* oracles in the book of Hosea? Who gathered them? How many editors (redactors) were there? When did *they* live, and what were the political, economic, and theological problems of their times? What did they hope to accomplish by expanding the manuscript of Hosea as they received it?

We will answer these questions, but there are two questions which we must answer first. There is a presupposition which runs throughout the book of Hosea from beginning to end. That presupposition is that Israel belongs to Yahweh in a special way, and Yahweh belongs to Israel in a special way. Because of this basic assumption, which underlies the entire book, there are two questions which we must answer before we can continue. The first question is "What was Israel?" and the second question is "Who was Yahweh?" In the next two chapters we will try to provide short but definitive answers.

CHAPTER II

What Was Israel?

There are several reasons why we must answer this question. For one thing there are several authors/editors of Hosea, and each one wrote at a different time in a distinct social setting. The name Israel did not have the same meaning for each author. Second, the eighth century prophets were conservative preachers who were grieving over old values of a former Israel which no longer existed, values which had been disgarded for various reasons by a society which had changed into something not imagined by the first champions of Yahweh. The first champions of Yahweh were members of a society which we will call proto-Israel, or pre-monarchical Israel. To understand the eighth century prophets we have to understand something about the early Israelites.

(A) PROTO-ISRAEL

> Then Joshua said to the House of Joseph, "You are a numerous people, and have great power; you shall not have one lot only, but the hill country shall be yours, for though it is a forest, you shall clear it and possess it to its furthest borders (Jos 17:17–18).

In the middle of the thirteenth century, around 1250 B.C.E., Israel first emerged as a self-conscious entity in the highlands of Canaan. The highlands consist of a string of mountains and mountainous areas running parallel to the Mediterranean sea-coast (which was to the west) and the Jordan River valley (to the east) in the land which was later called Palestine. The entire area, of which the highlands constitute a narrower strip, is only about sixty miles wide and three hundred to three hundred and fifty miles from north to south.

In the thirteenth century the population of the highlands increased dramatically. The area became densely peopled. There are various explanations for this population shift, both from the desert on the east, and the coastal plains on the west. Norman Gottwald in his massive book *The Tribes of Yahweh*[1] proposed a revolution of the lower classes, called marginal peoples, freeing themselves from the oppression of the Canaanite city-states which were located in a string from south to north in the area. These city-states were dependent on the farmers and herders who lived nearby for food, and on other nomadic groups for labor intensive activity and for soldiering. If necessary, marginal peoples (people living on the margins of a more affluent society) were forced into labor by whatever method was necessary. This social system has sometimes been called Canaanite feudalism, although some have objected to this terminology. Strong walled cities were ruled by political puppets of Egypt. They were petty rulers who were able to live comfortable lives, surrounded by friends and supporters who formed a cadre of control of the surrounding area.

There is a problem with the theory that a revolt, or revolution, produced proto-Israel. There is no historical evidence for this, nor is there any solid biblical support for such a profound upheaval. Surely a people like the ancient Israelites who kept many older traditions from the individual groups which joined the federation to become "Israel" would not have allowed a revolution to be ignored in the development of their traditions. It would not have been possible for the editors and scribes of Judah, who put together our Bible, to exclude a peasant revolt if it had taken place in Israel's past. We know that the compilers of the Old Testament were not adverse to including revolt themes in their compilations, as they did by including revolts led by Absalom, Jeroboam, and Jehu.

It is more likely that a social movement took place, something quite less than a revolt. It is probable that a new social entity emerged, and that this emergence became possible as a result of economic, political and military changes in Egypt which weakened the city-states and allowed large numbers of surrounding peasants to escape from areas where exploitation by more powerful and affluent groups was the rule.

The interest of Egypt in controlling the city-states had to do with trade and the maintenance of a military buffer zone. Palestine/Syria was a small area through which important trade routes ran between two powerful centers of civilization, Egypt, in northern Africa, to the southwest, and Mesopotamia (named for the Tigris and Euphrates Rivers) across the desert to the northeast. Controlling these city-states meant controlling this strategically important area. Egyptian soldiers spent much time subduing this area. Whatever turmoil transpired in Egypt during the thirteenth century, it caused the Canaanite city-state system of dominance in the area to deteriorate. This not only allowed Israel to emerge in the highlands independent of city-state control, but also allowed the sea people, the Philistines, to establish a foothold in the coastal area of Palestine.

So an agricultural federation of heterogeneous groups emerged which called itself Israel. The first groups which made up this federation were Canaanites (Amorites), 'Apiru mercenaries and adventurers (Hebrews), tribally organized farmers, nomads and transhumant pastoralists.[2]

From the start this federation was politically weak. The book of Judges gives us a picture of a people who lived next to each other without an overall political cohesion. There was a division between the north and the south also. When Judah joined the federation it was already a federation of smaller groups. There was always a division, north and south.

The groups which made up Israel are called tribes in the Bible. The Hebrew word is *shevet* (plural, *shevatim*). There were not twelve tribes in pre-monarchical Israel. The number twelve came later as a result of administrative decisions during the reigns of David and Solomon. It is believed that during the reign of David the entire area of the kingdom was divided into twelve areas so that each month of the year a "tribe" could be responsible for supplying food and other needs for the monarchy and its court. The divisions were revised for administrative reasons during the reign of Solomon:

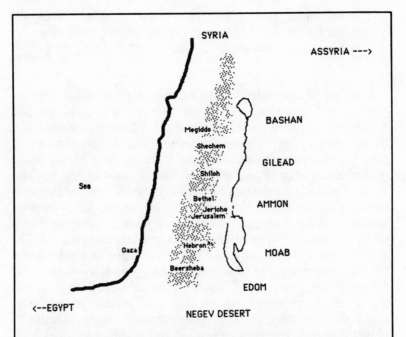

In the middle of the 13th century, Israel emerged in the highlands, a mountainous area running north and south from Galilee to the Negev, west of the Jordan valley, and east of the coastal plains of the Great Sea.

Some villages and cities which later became important in Israel are named in the above map.

Israel was a small nation surrounded by other small nations, each with its own god.

Solomon has twelve officers over all Israel, who provided food for the king and his household; each man
had to make provision for one month in the year (1
Kgs 4:7).

In the pre-monarchical period within each *shevet* (let's get
familiar with some Hebrew words) there were groups of families.
These groups were called *mishpahoth* (singular, *mishpahah*).
These groups of families are sometimes called clans. The *mishpahah* was a protective alliance of families. (The *shevet* was a
protective alliance of *mishpahoth*.) The alliance of families also
made it possible for the families to work together to share agricultural properties which were too expensive for one family to own,
and to share labor for extensive projects such as threshing floors,
terraces, wells, pools of laboring farm animals, and cisterns. The
alliance also made possible the sharing of risks; in a subsistence
farming community in an area like the highlands it was too risky
for a family to go it alone. Complete crop failure in any given area
was always a possibility. An alliance could arrange to have staggered planting, staggered harvests, and could accomplish this by
planting both at different elevations and at different times.[3]
    It is with the family that we have the truly basic unit of Israel
society, the intergenerational, extended family. This was the basic unit of society. There was no smaller unit. It was indivisible. It
was the producing and consuming social unit of society. It was
called a *beth-av* (plural, *bete-av,* and sometimes *bethoth*). It is my
belief that many of the later theological and ethical beliefs concerning the sacredness of the family in the Hebrew-Christian
ethical systems of the western world had their roots in the position of the *beth-av* in pre-monarchical Israel. The *beth-av* was the
central institution which was supported by the relationship of
itself to the other institutions of Israel.
    So we have three basic institutions to remember:
    1. *Beth-av* (intergenerational family)
    2. *Mishpahah* (coalition of families)
    3. *Shevet* (tribe)

The three layers of social institutions are seen in several

ancient traditions. For example, in the narrowing down of Israelites by Joshua to discover who had "broken faith in regard to devoted things," we read in Joshua:

> In the morning therefore you shall be brought near by
> your tribes; and the tribe (*shevet*) which the Lord takes
> shall come near by families (*mishpahoth*); and the family (*mishpahah*) which the Lord takes shall come near
> by households (7:14).

Another narrowing down takes place in one of the traditions concerning the selection of Saul as king in 1 Samuel:

> Then Samuel brought all the tribes of Israel near, and
> the tribe (*shevet*) of Benjamin was taken by lot. He
> brought the *shevet* of Benjamin near by its *mishpahoth,*
> and the *mishpahah* of the Matrites was taken by lot;
> finally he brought the family of the Matrites near man
> by man, and Saul the son of Kish was taken by lot
> (10:20–21).

For families largely dependent on subsistence farming for survival, the interconnectedness of beneficial social institutions was paramount. And although the groups forming proto-Israel enjoyed a great deal of independence, they had certain things in common.

COMMON CHARACTERISTICS OF THE SHEVATIM

1. They called the highlands their home.
2. They were all subsistence farmers.
3. They lived in a contiguous area.
4. They shared the same functional social institutions. It was the interconnectedness of these functional institutions which made survival possible. The *beth-av* was at the center, the survival of which was supported by the other institutions.
5. All members of proto-Israel were from the margins of society. All proto-Israel shared a feeling of being marginal. They

knew they were not the influential, the rich or the powerful. This is preserved for us in several scriptural traditions. Israel is not included in the Table of the Nations in Genesis 10 (an ancient table used by the Priestly editor/author in his compilation of Genesis), and in Deuteronomy 7:7 Israel is reminded:

> It was not because you were more in number than any other people that the Lord set his love upon you and chose you, for you were the fewest of all people (7:7).

In Numbers we have this interesting description:

> . . . a people dwelling alone, and not reckoning itself among the nations (23:8–9).

And we must not forget the plea in the book of Amos:

> How can Jacob stand? He is so small (7:2, 5).

6. They shared each other's traditions, eventually creating one body of tradition for all. The final tradition which emerged made them all Israelites, descendants of one family, children of Abraham, Isaac, and Jacob.

7. They had chosen Yahweh to be their God. Norman Gottwald in *The Tribes of Yahweh* calls the adoption and united devotion to the one God "mono-Yahwism." Mono-Yahwism was a functional theological belief which provided for these heterogeneous groups a cohesion which would not otherwise have been possible.[4] Behind the tradition of Joshua 24 is the exclusive choice of Yahweh as the God of Israel:

> Joshua said, ". . . put away the gods which your fathers served beyond the River, and in Egypt, and serve the Lord (Yahweh) . . . choose this day whom you will serve, whether the gods your fathers served in the region beyond the River, or the gods of the Amorites in whose land you dwell; but as for me and my house, we will serve the Lord (Yahweh)."

And the people said to Joshua, ". . . we will serve the Lord (Yahweh)." Then Joshua said to the people, "You are witnesses against yourselves that you have chosen the Lord, to serve him." And they said, "We are witnesses." He said, "Then put away foreign gods which are among you, and incline your heart to the Lord" (24:15–23).

With the background information supplied above concerning proto-Israel we have to reflect on the questions: "Who was Yahweh?" "What kind of a God was Yahweh, and why was he chosen by the *shevatim* of pre-monarchical Israel?" We will answer these questions in Chapter III.

Before doing that there are several periods in Israel's subsequent history which we must identify.

(B) THE UNITED KINGDOM

For approximately one hundred years during the tenth century, Israel was the name of a people who claimed as their kings Saul, David, and Solomon. During this period Israel included both the north (later called Israel and sometimes Ephraim) and the south, Judah.

(C) AFTER SOLOMON'S DEATH

From 922 until 722 B.C.E., including the period of the eighth century, when Hosea and Amos prophesied, Israel was the area of the pre-monarchical federation, minus the southern area of Judah.

(D) AFTER 722 B.C.E., A NATION WHICH NO LONGER EXISTED

The Assyrians relocated much of the population of Israel to the east and moved into the area of Israel another population foreign to the area. The poor remained. They were not relocated. Some of the Israelites fled to the southern kingdom of Judah. They took with them many northern traditions and northern

**METAPHORS FOR ISRAEL IN THE BOOK OF HOSEA
BY CHAPTER AND VERSE**

CHAPTER/VERSE	METAPHOR
2:2	MOTHER
2:2ff.	WIFE
2:4b	HARLOT
2:7a	HARLOT
4:16	A STUBBORN HEIFER
5:13	A SICK PERSON
7:8	A CAKE NOT TURNED
7:9	GRAY HAIRED MAN
7:11	A SILLY DOVE
7:16	A SLACK BOW
8:8	A USELESS VESSEL
8:9	A WILD ASS
9:10	GRAPES IN THE WILDERNESS
9:10	FIRST FRUIT ON FIG TREE
9:16	DRIED UP FRUIT TREE
10:1	A LUXURIANT VINE
10:11	TRAINED HEIFER
11:1	A CHILD, A SON
12:7a	DISHONEST MERCHANT
13:3	MORNING MIST OR DEW
13:3	CHAFF THAT SWIRLS
13:3	SMOKE FROM A WINDOW
13:5–8	A HERD IN DANGER
13:13	AN UNBORN SON
14:5	A LILY
14:5–6	A HEALTHY POPLAR TREE
14:7	A GARDEN, A VINE

There are over 26 metaphors for Israel in the book of Hosea. The wife
and son have captured the imagination of readers through the centuries.

Compare this chart with the chart entitled
"Metaphors in Hosea for Israel/Ephraim" by author.

ways of looking at their religious history. The spiritual descendants of those who fled to the south, including levitical priests of Shiloh/Shechem, gave birth to the Deuteronomists of seventh century Judah.

(E) DURING THE DAYS OF JOSIAH

At the end of the seventh century, because Assyria was in severe political, military, and economic decline, Josiah was able to attempt the annexation of the territory to the north, formerly Israel.

> And in the cities of Manasseh, Ephraim, and Simeon, and as far as Naphtali, in their ruins round about, he [Josiah] broke down the altars, and beat the Asherim and the images into powder, and hewed down all the incense altars throughout all the land of Israel (2 Chr 34:6–7).

(F) DURING THE EXILE, AFTER THE DESTRUCTION OF JUDAH

An interesting change took place in the exilic community regarding the name Israel. The name of Israel was revived as an alternate name for Judah. There are many examples of this change of meaning. The south became known by the ancient, pre-monarchical name Israel:

> So you, son of man, I have made a watchman for the house of Israel (Ez 33:7).

> . . . they shall call you the City of the Lord, the Zion of the Holy One of Israel (Is 60:14).

> And the people of Israel, the priests and the Levites, and the rest of the returned exiles, celebrated the dedication of this house of God with joy (Ezr 6:16).

We said at the end of Chapter I that the book of Hosea is a book about the relationship between Israel and Yahweh. It is for this reason that we are answering the two complementary questions: "What was Israel?" and "Who was Yahweh?" There is another distinction that we should make at this time before moving on to Yahweh. Yahweh is never called the God of the Israelites. He is called the God of Israel hundreds of times (*Tribes,* p. 240). The point I am making here is that Israel was an institution like the *shevet, mishpahah,* and *beth-av.* Israel was the coalition of the *shevatim.* It will be helpful in understanding the relationship between Yahweh and Israel if we remember that individualism, characteristic of our post-industrial age and common in the western world since the renaissance, did not exist in early Israel in any form. The identity of an individual was completely absorbed in the group to which he or she belonged. Later, after the eighth century, a concept emerged which allowed Judahites to think in terms of partial groups, smaller sections of the entire group. This concept is the remnant. Our examination of the book of Amos led us to conclude that Amos of Tekoa (the prophet of justice) did not employ the concept of the remnant in his oracles. We will find that Hosea also was not able to think in terms of a smaller group within Israel. When the representatives of the nation sinned, everyone was held responsible.

In subsequent chapters we will examine the perception of Israel by the several editors and authors of the book of Hosea. Now we turn to the vital pre-monarchical understanding of Israel's chosen God, Yahweh. We will also look at some of the changes which later took place in the life of Israel/Judah and how these changes affected the perception of Yahweh.

CHAPTER III

Who Was Yahweh?

PRE-MONARCHICAL PERCEPTIONS OF YAHWEH

The first god of Israel was El. El was a high god of the Canaanites, and the earliest Israelites were Canaanites. But El was a god of the status quo; he was aloof, far removed, and he stood for something that the status quo liked: orderliness.

El was not the ideal god for the people called Israel, because El didn't take sides. Israel needed a god suited for marginal people, a god who would fight for them against the status quo if necessary. The early federation found out about the kind of God they needed when the "Moses" tribes moved into the highlands and joined the federation. The "Moses" tribes were the Hebrews. The Hebrews were a social class of people who gave meaning to the word "marginal." They existed outside the "respectable" circles of society. Before this group of Hebrews joined Israel they had no place to call their own, no property of their own. Their equals today would be migrant laborers from Mexico working in Texas or California for slave wages, forced to live in squalor. A social class called Hebrews continued to exist in Palestine/Syria long after this particular group of Hebrews joined Israel. They are mentioned as mercenaries hired to fight for the Philistines.

> Now the Hebrews who had been with the Philistines
> before that time and who had gone up with them into
> the camp, even they also turned to be with the Israelites
> who were with Saul and Jonathan (1 Sam 14:21).

The "Moses" group of Hebrews had worked on building projects in Egypt for subsistence, and as time went by they were

23

forced into slavery. When they decided to move on they found out that they were prisoners of the Egyptian state. They had needed someone to fight for them, for their liberation, and they found a fighter/God in Yahweh.

> Yahweh was a man of war (Ex 15:3).

> Yahweh will fight for you and you have only to be still (Ex 14:14).

> The Lord God who goes before you will himself fight for you (Deut 1:30).

Yahweh led them out of Egypt. When they arrived in Israel, Yahweh arrived with them.

Many early traditions of Yahweh present a very human (anthropomorphic) God. When he wages war, he wages war like a crafty warrior. When the Egyptians followed the Israelites through the sea bed,

> Yahweh . . . looked down upon the hosts of the Egyptians, and discomfited the hosts of the Egyptians, clogging (or removing) their chariot wheels . . . and the Egyptians said, "Let us flee from before Israel; for Yahweh fights for them against the Egyptians" (Ex 14:24–25).

In Joshua 24 Yahweh reminds Israel how he dealt with the two kings of the Amorites:

> And I sent the Hornet before you, which drove them out before you, the two kings of the Amorites; it was not by your sword or by your bow (24:12).

At a later time, when the Philistines captured the ark of the tabernacle (believed to be the throne of Yahweh) the men of the city were stricken by Yahweh with tumors. An Old English translation adds, "in their secret parts" (1 Sam 5:9).

There are numerous passages which show just how human Yahweh was. When the J author of Genesis (who lived in Jerusalem during the united kingdom) wrote about Yahweh walking in the garden of Eden he even had his footsteps making noise.

> And they [Adam and Eve] heard the sound of Yahweh God walking in the garden in the cool of the day (Gen 3:8).

And just to give one further example, in the Deuteronomic law of the clean camp, the soldiers are told to keep the camp clean so as not to offend Yahweh.

> Because Yahweh your God walks in the midst of your camp, to save you and to give up your enemies before you, therefore your camp must be holy, that he may not see anything indecent among you, and turn away from you (Deut 23:14).

Making a pact with Yahweh was a calculated risk. Yahweh was a great warrior, but he did have his limitations. He was limited in the scope of his activity. Although he seems to have needed little or no sleep, he did seem to have been limited in his presence to one place at a time. He was not omnipresent, and there are many references to Yahweh arriving on the scene. For example, a stirring, warlike description of Yahweh appears in the Song of Deborah. Recognized by scholars as ancient, Yahweh is described as "marching" out of the south.

> Lord [Yahweh], when thou didst go forth from Seir
>   when thou didst march from the region of Edom,
> the earth trembled,
>   and the heavens dropped,
>   yea, the clouds dropped water.
> The mountains quaked before Yahweh,
>   yon Sinai before Yahweh, the god of Israel (Jgs 5:4–5).

In some stories the presence of Yahweh seemed to be limited to the location of the ark of the covenant.

"Let us bring the ark of the covenant of Yahweh here from Shiloh, that he may come among us and save us from the power of our enemies." ... When the ark of the covenant of Yahweh came into the camp, all Israel gave a mighty shout, so that the earth resounded (1 Sam 4:3–5).

Also, Yahweh had a temper. And he could lose his temper:

And the people complained in the hearing of Yahweh about their misfortunes; and when Yahweh heard it, his anger was kindled, and the fire of Yahweh burned among them, and consumed some outlying parts of the camp (Num 11:1).

But Yahweh could be influenced to calm down.

Then the people cried to Moses; and Moses prayed to Yahweh, and the fire abated (Num 2:2).

And Yahweh was concerned about his reputation. In Numbers there is a story about Moses reminding Yahweh what will happen to his reputation if he punishes the Israelites.

And Yahweh said to Moses, ". . . I will strike them with the pestilence and disinherit them. . . ." But Moses said to Yahweh, "Then the Egyptians will hear of it. . . . Then the nations who have heard of thy fame will say, 'Because Yahweh was not able to bring this people into the land which he swore to give them, therefore he has slain them in the wilderness.' " . . . Then Yahweh said, "I have pardoned according to your word" (Num 14:11–20).

The wilderness tradition developed over a long period of time, and may not have been the tradition of the "Moses" tribes originally. There are many pieces of it which we cannot deal with in this short summary. There are some scholars who find three distinct traditions in the tetrateuch—an exodus tradition, a Sinai tradition, and a wilderness tradition. How the three became merged is a book in itself.[1]

We believe that in early Israel a group entering the coalition was enthusiastic about the good reputation which Yahweh earned by freeing them (the Hebrews) from the Egyptians, and convinced enough Israelites to adopt Yahweh as their official God. I have chosen my words carefully. Notice that I did not say that Yahweh chose Israel. I believe that the concept of Yahweh choosing Israel developed later in the nation's development, perhaps during the united kingdom period, but in greater detail and with more purpose, in Judah during the late seventh century.

We have already mentioned the tradition of adopting Yahweh in Joshua 24. Joshua challenges the people:

> Choose this day whom you will serve, whether the gods
> your fathers served in the region beyond the River, or
> the gods of the Amorites in whose land you dwell; but as
> for me and my house, we will serve Yahweh (24:15).

Behind this tradition is a true happening, the details of which we may never know. It is not likely that the champions of Yahweh had the support of all the people. Under the circumstances it is not likely that a small group of leaders, or even a large group of leaders, would have been able to make a religious decision (although in fact it was also a political decision) which would be acceptable to all the citizens. I am sure that many did not stop worshiping El, the god which we have called the first god of Israel. Later in the history of the nation the attributes of El and Yahweh would be combined, and the names of the two entirely different gods would be used interchangeably for one God.

The important point I would like to make here is that Yahweh was the kind of God you could become enthusiastic about. He was nearby. He was reliable. His character resembled the character of the marginal people whose causes he championed. He would gain a reputation as a winner who preferred the lower classes of society, an element which needed him more than the politically powerful of the nations. After all, the nations had large professional armies, with central control, chariots, horses, swords and weapons. They didn't need, or perhaps wouldn't want to trust, a god to fight for them. They trusted in their own military and political strength and skill.

> Some boast of chariots, and some of horses;
>> But we boast of the name of Yahweh our God (Ps 20:7).

An author of Hosea condemned his own people Israel.

> Because you have trusted in your chariots,
>> and in the multitudes of your warriors,
> therefore the tumult of war shall arise among your people,
>> and all your fortresses shall be destroyed. . . .
> Thus it shall be done to you, O house of Israel (Hos
>> 10:13–15).

There are several things we know. One of them is that Yahweh was a God you could get excited about, and we also know that Yahweh always had his champions among the Israelites.

PERCEPTIONS OF YAHWEH IN JOSIANIC TIMES

In this book we are taking the viewpoint that a major redaction of the book of Hosea took place during the reign of Josiah, at the time when the first edition of the Deuteronomistic History appeared. For this reason we must examine the theological perceptions of Yahweh which were current at that time in Jerusalem. There are limitations to our attempt to understand Israel's perceptions of Yahweh.

    a. There were territorial differences.
    b. There were competing viewpoints.
    c. No one was in charge.

Above we tried to describe, using some detail, the relationship between Yahweh and Israel during the pre-monarchical period. We have a large body of tradition about this period. And that is part of the problem. The Old Testament began to take its canonical form following the destruction of Jerusalem in 587, and although the first edition of the Deuteronomistic History appeared during the reign of Josiah, and used some ancient traditions, Josiah lived almost four hundred years after the end of the pre-monarchical period. The seventh century Israelite/Judahite view of the early, pre-monarchical period was far removed from the actual facts. One of the views of the early relations between Yahweh and Israel is summarized by the word "covenant." Scholars tell us that a covenant, patterned after the form of a Hittite vassal treaty (a treaty between a superior military force and a weaker political entity, supposedly for the benefit of both parties), had been established between Israel and Yahweh. We are further told that the eighth century prophets grieved over the deterioration of this covenantal relationship, and that underlying their oracles is a firm idea of the breaking of the covenant.

Unfortunately the word covenant is one of the most deadly words in the English language. It is a word which adds heavy structure to what was probably a live, exciting relationship between Yahweh and Israel in those ancient times before the monarchy. We are indebted to the Deuteronomists of the late seventh century for beginning our Bible history and for rescuing the eighth century prophets from obscurity, but we have had to pay a price. Too many of us have bought the D projection into the distant past of a structured vassal treaty relationship (which in some embryonic way may even have existed), thus clouding our own vision of the vitality of religion before the monarchy.

Let's free ourselves of this feeling we have had thrust on us by scholars for centuries, that in order to understand the Old Testament we have to understand the full meaning of the word "covenant." In this book we will follow the practice of avoiding the word and the concept as long as possible, at least until our discussion of the Josianic period. The idea of a structured covenant was big among the Deuteronomists of the seventh century, but for us to project the concept back into an earlier period is counter-productive. Yahweh in early Israel was simply not a covenant-loving God. He was a God suited for pre-monarchical Israel, and he was faithful to the federation. A relationship existed between the federation, but we can only speculate on the exact nature of that relationship. We don't know if the majority of the people joined into the relationship in some way, and we don't even know in what sense the relationship was official, and what role the traditions of the past (like Sinai/Horeb) played in early Israel.

During the reign of King Josiah, in the late seventh century, the importance of writing and the production of written documents moved the people of Judah, including the descendants of refugees from the north, in the direction of unity in national purpose and theological understanding.

We stated earlier that as time passed, the characteristics of Yahweh as warrior and champion of Israel merged with loftier concepts of El, the high god of the Canaanites. The anthropomorphic (human) immanence of Yahweh diminished and the distance of a high God took over.

An early change in the role of Yahweh can be seen in those stories which tell of the spirit of Yahweh coming upon a hero, enabling the hero to deliver Israel.

But the spirit of Yahweh took possession of Gideon (Jgs 6:34).

Then the spirit of Yahweh came upon Jephthah (Jgs 11:29).

And behold a young lion roared against him [Samson]; and the spirit of Yahweh came mightily upon him, and he tore the lion asunder as one tears a kid; and he had nothing in his hand (Jgs 14:6).

And the spirit of Yahweh came mightily upon David from that day forward (1 Sam 16:13).

Instead of Yahweh himself fighting for the people, these passages indicate that humans were empowered to carry out the same role. However this empowerment came to an end in the Deuteronomistic History rather early. After the spirit of Yahweh came on David, it never came on anyone else in the same "empowering" way. With the establishment of the monarchy, Yahweh quietly and quickly became a worker behind the scenes.

Richard Elliot Friedman in his book *The Exile and Biblical Narrative*[2] writes:

> At several junctures the immanence of YHWH seems to diminish. DTR pictures Israel's early history as the events of an age of power, a time in which YHWH is seen to be clearly and regularly immanent in the life of the people . . . appearing among them, and producing public miraculous events as signs and wonders. Nearly all of these marks of that age of power, however, begin to diminish early in DTR and completely disappear from the account early in the portrayal of the monarchy (p. 37).

In the first edition of the Deuteronomistic History we should note the following. The last appearance of Yahweh to a human is to King Solomon. The last important public miracle is in the Elijah cycle. The last mention of the appearance of the *kabod* (glory) of Yahweh is at the dedication of the temple in 1 Kings 8.

Three hundred years after Solomon, during the reign of Josiah, the amazingly zealous circle of levitical priests and scribes emerged, the members of which we call the Deuteronomists. (They never called themselves by this name.) The values of this school can be seen in the person of Josiah himself. Josiah is the cumulative hero of the entire first edition of the Deuteronomistic History. This edition of the history starts with Moses and ends with Josiah. If we understand this hero Josiah, we understand the late seventh century theological perception of Yahweh. In the Josianic edition of DH the hero is the individual who systematically and conscientiously consults and lives by the torah of Yahweh. This is what pleases Yahweh, and this is what ensures victory over one's enemies. Yahweh was now perceived as a highly structured, distant God whose ancient proclamations were sacred and whose ordinances, statutes and laws served as a guide to victory and survival for his people. Rather than an intimate God who personally became involved in the battles of his people, Yahweh was regarded as one who had a long-standing formal, treaty-like relationship with his people. This formal covenant relationship was projected into Israel's distant past by the Deuteronomists who believed that this theological perspective was the one which would work to preserve the nation in a chaotic world of shifting military powers. As has been well established, Yahweh no longer dwelt in the temple; only his *name* dwelt in the central shrine.

We have preserved for us in Solomon's dedicatory prayer of the temple two perceptions of Yahweh from two stages of Israel's history. On the one hand Solomon says:

> Yahweh has set the sun in the heavens,
>   but has said that he would dwell in thick darkness.
> I have built for thee an exalted house,
>   a place for thee to dwell in for ever (1 Kgs 8:12–13).

Immediately thereafter Solomon is reported to have prayed a prayer filled with Deuteronomistic language in which he says:

> But will God indeed dwell on the earth? Behold, heaven
> and the highest heaven cannot contain thee; how much
> less this house which I have built (1 Kgs 8:27).

The lofty view of a distant Yahweh whose name dwelt in the central shrine at Jerusalem, whose chief pleasure was that his people observe his statutes and ordinances and continue to observe his structured covenant, was only a step to a much loftier view of Yahweh which would emerge in the following century.

PERCEPTIONS OF YAHWEH IN EXILE

The Josianic dream of the Deuteronomists came to a tragic end when King Josiah went to Megiddo to encounter Pharaoh Neco, king of Egypt, and was killed in battle. King Josiah's body was returned to Jerusalem and buried, and along with it the seventh century version of the Deuteronomic theology. The Deuter-onomistic History after Josiah has its own characteristics which identify it as an addendum to the greater work. Its content is all downhill. It ends inconclusively.

What happened to the salvation of Yahweh? Was he impo-tent, angry, vindictive, or was there some method to his mad-ness? Was Judah destroyed because Yahweh had lost interest or lacked the power to save his people? The exilic answer to these theological questions was amazing. The destruction of Judah was viewed as a manifestation of Yahweh's will and a fulfillment of his word.

As time went on in the exilic community, faith triumphed over despair. The growth of an optimistic faith, the kind of faith that sometimes grows paradoxically in times of great adversity, bolstered by various problems for the conquering Babylonians, problems concerning internal economic, military, and political developments, resulted in a religion for Yahweh's people per-meated with hope. Old men began to dream dreams, and young men began to see visions. A new and powerful interest in the old tradition of Israel concerning the exodus became the center for new and glorious oracles of a new prophet whose name we do not know, but whose poetry became an extension of the book of Isaiah. As if the Judahites were ashamed and guilty for having doubted the power of Yahweh during the early days of captivity, they developed a new appreciation of his power, a power which now reached in so many directions that it could only be described as universal, and reached back in time to the days of creation. Here are some of the specifics of exilic faith:

a. One momentous result of the captivity period was a phe-nomenon which was going to influence the history of civilization for thousands of years. The captives, deprived of their king and their freedom, the city of Jerusalem and the temple, learned to treasure the one thing they were able to take with them to Baby-lon—their religious writings. These writings, some of which would become "holy" scriptures for millions of people in the future, were read, searched, studied, memorized and adored. Some of the scrolls would be expanded and updated. Several of these scrolls were based on the oracles of the eighth century prophets, including Hosea, Amos, Micah, and Isaiah. The word of Yahweh became precious.

b. A compassionate side of Yahweh's nature emerged, introduced by the words of Deutero-Isaiah,

"Comfort, comfort my people," says your God. . . .
He will feed his flock like a shepherd,
   he will gather the lambs in his arms,
He will carry them in his bosom,
   and gently lead those that are with young.

He gives power to the faint,
      and to him who has no might
      he increases strength (Is 40:1, 11, 29).

c. Yahweh was perceived as having a new involvement with nature extending back to creation itself.

Why do you say O Jacob,
   and speak, O Israel,
"My way is hid from the Lord,
   and my right is disregarded by my God"?
Have you not known?
   Have you not heard?
Yahweh is the everlasting God,
   the creator of the ends of the earth (Is 40:27–28).

Although no longer perceived as an intimate God, Yahweh's aloofness was going to enable him to control more than the going out and coming in of Israel. From the midst of the least of all people, Israel in exile, Yahweh was now perceived as the almighty one, not only for Israel, but for the whole world. When Israel returned to rebuild the temple of Yahweh, as they definitely would, the rebuilt temple would not only be the dwelling place for the name of Yahweh, but also a house of prayer:

For my house shall be called a house of prayer for all peoples (Is 56:7).

CHAPTER IV

Problems in the Book of Hosea and a Solution

There are problems in the book of Hosea which confront every reader and need our attention. These include abrupt changes in mood and viewpoint illustrated by passages of severe judgment followed immediately by passages of salvation and hope. Another problem has to do with changes of person in oracles which seem to have unity. The third problem is one which the average student will not be aware of until he or she notices the footnotes in the Revised Standard Version. This third problem is called corruption of the text. We will discuss these problems briefly in this chapter with additional information later.

ABRUPT CHANGES FROM ORACLES OF JUDGMENT TO ORACLES OF SALVATION

Early in our reading of Hosea we encounter the problem of changing viewpoints, diametrically opposed statements concerning the fate of the people of Yahweh. In chapter one, immediately after reading about the names of the three children, Jezreel, Not Pitied, and Not My People (all three of which are related to severe punishment for Israel), we read the following:

> Yet the number of the people of Israel shall be like the sand of the sea, which can be neither measured nor numbered; and in the place where it was said to them, "You are not my people," it shall be said to them, "Sons of the living God." And the people of Judah and the people of Israel shall be gathered together, and they

shall appoint for themselves one head; and they shall go
up from the land, for great shall be the day of Jezreel.
　　Say to your brother, "My people," and to your sister,
"She has obtained pity" (Hos 1:10–2:1).

Another change is noted in 2:13–14 where punishment is
again followed by grace and mercy:

And I will punish her for the feast days of the Baals
　　when she burned incense to them.
and decked herself with her ring and jewelry,
　　and went after her lovers,
　　and forgot me, says the Lord.
Therefore, behold, I will allure her,
　　and bring her into the wilderness,
　　and speak tenderly to her.
And there I will give her her vineyards,
　　and make the valley of Achor a door of hope.

CHANGES OF PERSON

Changes of person can be seen in an address to, or concerning, the wife.

And in that day, says the Lord, *you* will call me, "My
husband," and no longer will *you* call me, "My Baal."
For I will remove the names of the Baals from *her*
mouth (Hos 2:16; italics mine).

Earlier in chapter 2 the children are addressed in the second
person imperative ("Plead with your mother, plead") and a sentence later are referred to in the third person ("Upon her children
also I will have no pity").
　　A change in person is routinely considered by scholars to be
a sign of an addition to a previously established text. The scribe
making the addition, a comment or an editorial remark either
does not feel that it is necessary to use the same person, or is
unaware of his syntactical error.

A CORRUPT TEXT

This means at least two things: (a) The oldest and best manuscripts which we have for the book of Hosea do not agree in many places, and applying the best principles of textual criticism has not provided scholars with agreement as to what the original text said. (b) The rules of biblical Hebrew as we understand them don't seem to apply in several places.

We include this information concerning the state of the text because the student should be aware of it. There are some passages in the book about which we cannot reach dogmatic conclusions. This has not discouraged a host of fine scholars from studying the book, and it should not discourage us, even if some of our conclusions must be tentative.

SOLUTIONS

There are two things we can do to increase our appreciation of the book of Hosea and resolve or reduce the effect of the "problems" referred to above. The first is to understand scribal commentary as practiced in ancient Israel beginning in the seventh century. The second is to modify our approach to the book.

SCRIBAL COMMENTARY

Some of the problems with the book of Hosea are evidence of the process involved in the evolution of the book and show the hands of several authors. It is important to remember that there was no doctrine concerning the sacredness or verbal inspiration of written documents until after the exile. By this time (the restoration of Israel in Judah) books such as Hosea and Amos were complete. They had reached their canonical form. To this final edition we would not dare to add or subtract, or alter in any way. But the process by which they reached their final form is discoverable to us today. We must accept the facts as they present themselves and try to understand them. In earlier times in Israel there was no one version of local traditions. Local traditions were just that. They varied from locale to locale. No one was in charge of traditions, saying that one version was true and all other versions were wrong. The first move to standardization came when the local traditions were committed to writing, a great deal of which was produced in the days of King Josiah by zealous Levites, supporters of centralization and unification in Judah, a group we call the Deuteronomists.

Later, during the exile, when the Judahites were deprived of their temple and Jerusalem, the writings (the only things they had) became sacred. They were read, studied, expanded, memorized, and adored.

> Oh, how I love thy law!
> > It is my meditation all the day. . . .
> Thy word is a lamp to my feet
> > and a light to my path. . . .
> Thy testimonies are wonderful;
> > therefore my soul keeps them.
> The unfolding of thy words gives light;
> > it imparts understanding to the simple.
> With open mouth I pant,
> > because I long for thy commandments (Ps 119:97, 105, 129–131).

Before the final edition of a book developed, there was a process of growth involving one or more steps. The scribes producing new editions of previously written material realized that the problems of an earlier Israel (a hundred years or more before) were not the same as the age in which they lived. Realizing how valuable the older material was, an updating process was engaged in whereby the scribe, who was a theologian in his own right, would add commentary to an older text. Although there are many examples of this practice, none is more evident than the commentary of two scribes found in the middle of the ten commandments. We refer to the two statements of commentary made by the priestly author and the Deuteronomistic author after the commandment concerning the sabbath day. In Exodus we read one comment on the purpose of the sabbath, and in Deuteronomy a completely different commentary. Compare:

> For in six days the Lord made the heavens and the earth, the sea, and all that is in them, and rested the seventh day; therefore the Lord blessed the sabbath day and hallowed it (Ex 20:11).

> You shall remember that you were a servant in the land of Egypt, and the Lord your God brought you out thence with a mighty hand and an outstretched arm; therefore the Lord your God commanded you to keep the sabbath day (Deut 5:15).

These explanations could not both be part of the ten commandments. They are two comments representing two different theological viewpoints. Our purpose in looking at these explanations is to become aware of scribal commentary. Here it is easy to identify. In Hosea there is a great deal of commentary, sentences and fragments of sentences added to a previous edition. Where did the scribes get the authority to add these comments? Actually it was the most natural thing in their world to do this.

We have to remember that "individualism" (or pride of individual accomplishment) was not a characteristic known in Israel. It did not exist. Authors of books (scrolls) did not include their names in their scrolls. They did not expect to own them; they belonged to Israel.

Today, living in an entirely different age, a book is considered the "property" of the author. Subsequent editors add comment to reproduced books, usually in the form of footnotes at the bottom of the page or in the rear of the book. Even the Bible itself has been printed with commentary in this fashion many times in the last few decades by persons and organizations who have no intention of altering the Bible, but whose purpose is to add clarity to it. We can argue about the success or failure of this practice, but if so-called "Bible believers" have done it after the establishment of the sacred canon, why do we find scribal comment a strange practice before the finalization of the canon? In the next chapter we will identify the author who produced the first written manuscript of Hosea, and the two subsequent redactors (editors/authors/scribes), and try to understand their theological motivation.

MODIFYING OUR APPROACH TO THE BOOK

Persons reading the book of Hosea sometimes get a fragmented feeling because of the lack of logical development. The truth is that the book of Hosea is not written with systematic linear logic. If a reader expects logical development I recommend that the following question be asked: Is there another way to read the book? Logic was the gift of the Greeks, and we are in love with logic in our age of science. But logic was never a greatly valued or developed characteristic in ancient Israel.

Instead of expecting logical development I suggest that we read the book of Hosea as a work of art. Art has its own logic. Take for example a score of great music. Themes are introduced according to the composer's judgment, sometimes briefly to be developed later. Sometimes themes are placed back-to-back in contrast to each other to produce an emotional reaction, to heighten the response of the hearers, and to communicate truth in a non-verbal way. I suggest that we read the book of Hosea as a musical composition consisting of an overture and two movements. In the overture the themes are introduced briefly, to be developed later. The overture and both movements end with the theme of Israel returning home:

> Afterward the children of Israel shall return and seek the Lord their God, and David their king (3:5).

> They shall come trembling like birds from Egypt, and like doves from the land of Assyria; and I will return them to their homes, says the Lord (11:11).

They shall return and dwell beneath my shadow, they
shall flourish as a garden (14:7).

Other themes include the theme of the husband and wife,
the theme of the father and son, the theme of punishment, and
the theme of salvation. Many scholars have noted an artistic
unity of the first section of Hosea (chapters 1 to 3). We now turn
to the growth of this powerful prelude to the oracles of Hosea.

CHAPTER V

The Allegory of the Bad Marriage

CHAPTERS 1 TO 3

The book of Hosea is divided into three sections. Almost everybody identifies section I as containing chapters 1 to 3. A popular way to divide the remainder of the book is Section II: chapters 4–11, and Section III: chapters 12–14. H.W. Wolff divides the book of Hosea in this way:[1]

> Section I Chapters 1–3
> Section II Chapters 4–11
> Section III Chapters 12–14

With this division each section begins with an accusation.

> . . . the land commits great harlotry by forsaking the Lord (1:2).

> . . . the Lord has a controversy with the inhabitants of the land. There is no faithfulness or kindness, and no knowledge of God in the land (4:1).

> . . . they multiply falsehood and violence . . . The Lord has an indictment against Judah, and will punish Jacob according to his ways (12:1–2).

And each section ends with the Israelites returning.

> Afterward the children of Israel shall return and seek the Lord their God, and David their king (3:5).

They shall come trembling like birds from Egypt, and like doves from the land of Assyria; and I will return them to their homes, says the Lord (11:11).

They shall return and dwell beneath my shadow, they shall flourish as a garden (14:7).

A REDACTIONAL FORM-CRITICAL APPROACH TO HOSEA

In the opinion of some scholars there are some slight variations to the above three part division.[2] However the important thing to remember, even if we alter the divisions, is this: *Each section of the book of Hosea contains several levels of authorship.*

In our last chapter we highlighted some of the problems associated with the book of Hosea. Any hypothesis which seeks to explain the book must grapple with, and if possible solve, these problems. For this book we have chosen a well worked out hypothesis of a recent book entitled *Composition and Tradition in the Book of Hosea, A Redactional Critical Investigation* by Gale A. Yee, based on her dissertation.[3]

There are several reasons why we chose Dr. Yee's hypothesis, based on a four-levels-of-authorship approach to the development of Hosea. First, it grapples with and solves the problems discussed in the previous chapter. Second, it makes sense, considering what we know of the development of written religious documents in Judah during the days of Josiah, and the subsequent exploding importance of written documents in the exilic community. Third, it is based on a thorough linguistic analysis of what we know to be the practices of Judaistic scribes in the Josianic and exilic period. (See Appendix.)

THE CHRONOLOGY OF THE DEVELOPMENT
OF THE BOOK OF HOSEA

Before we isolate the oracles of Hosea as the first step in reconstructing the development of chapters 1 to 3, we will summarize the chronology of our chosen hypothesis.

CHRONOLOGY FOR THE DEVELOPMENT OF
THE BOOK OF HOSEA

AUTHOR/ EDITOR	TIME FRAME	PROBABLE LOCATION
HOSEA	FINAL DAYS OF ISRAEL 760–735	ISRAEL (The Northern Kingdom)
COLLECTOR	AFTER FALL OF ISRAEL REIGN OF HEZEKIAH 716–687	JUDAH
JOSIANIC REDACTOR	DURING THE REIGN OF JOSIAH (Time of DTR 1)	JERUSALEM
EXILIC REDACTOR	DURING THE EXILE (Time of DTR 2)	BABYLON

(1) Hosea prophesied during the final days of Israel (750–722). Another guess as to the exact years of Hosea's oracles would be 760–735.

(2) Following the fall of Israel the oracles of Hosea were written down by a person called the collector. This was probably an Israelite who fled to Judah. This may have happened during the reign of Hezekiah (716–687).

(3) In the days of Josiah (640–609) a Josianic redactor of the Deuteronomistic circle used the collection of Hosea's oracles mentioned above to produce a book which would bring to the people living in the days of Josiah the value of Hosea's oracles while at the same time supporting the Deuteronomistic goals. (Redactors also did this with the collections of other eighth century prophets.)

(4) During the exile (sixth century) an exilic redactor, an heir of the Deuteronomistic values of the previous century, enlarged the Josianic edition of Hosea and produced the canonical

book, the book of Hosea in its final form. We assume that this exilic redactor lived in Babylon, but he may have lived in Judah or even Egypt.

DEVELOPMENT OF SECTION I, CHAPTERS 1 TO 3

We will start first by identifying the oracles of Hosea and then explain how they were transferred and reinterpreted by changing events in the life of Israel. At each step of the way the original oracles found themselves in a new environment and a new framework. The growth of this framework is the real subject of this book. We follow the passages identified by Dr. Gale Yee in her book.

THE ORACLES OF HOSEA BEN BEERI

The original oracles of Hosea are located throughout the book of Hosea, starting with these words:

Plead with your mother, plead (2:4a)

and continue to appear, scattered throughout the book, ending with the words:

Samaria shall bear her guilt,
    because she has rebelled against her God;
They will fall by the sword,
        their little ones shall be dashed in pieces.
        and their pregnant women ripped open (13:16).

In Section I (chapters 1 to 3) the oracles of Hosea are these:

Plead with your mother, plead—
    that she put away her harlotry from her face,
    and her adultery from between her breasts;
lest I strip her naked
    and make her as in the day she was born,
and make her like a wilderness,

and set her like a parched land,
and slay her with thirst (2:2–3).

For she said, "I will go after my lovers,
who gave me my bread and my water,
my wool and my flax, my oil and my drink" (2:5b).

Now I will uncover her lewdness in the sight of her lovers,
and no one shall rescue her out of my hand (2:10).

In order to understand the implications of our chosen hypothesis and to view its development, there are several facts about the oracles of Hosea which we should note. Since at this time we are examining only chapters 1 to 3, we will list six facts about the original oracles. In Chapter VI entitled "The Oracles of Hosea," we will expand this list to include ten facts.

(1) The name of Hosea does not appear in his oracles. This is true of all oracles of eighth century prophets. When the name of the prophet appears, it is a later addition of an editor.

(2) Yahweh is often the speaker. In later oracles of Hosea, Yahweh identifies himself by name (12:9).

(3) Who are the addressees? From chapter 4 on all oracles are addressed to the rulers of Israel in Samaria. Who then is addressed in the first oracle which says:

"Plead with your mother, plead"? I believe that this opening oracle may be a primitive prophetic call. It may be addressed to Hosea.

(4) Who is the mother? The mother can be the nation Israel, or the capital city of Samaria, where decisions are made. Yee says that Rachel, the mother of Joseph and Benjamin, is the mother. She bases this partly on the closing oracles of Hosea where Jacob is identified as the father. Rachel was Jacob's favorite wife.

(5) There is nothing about Gomer in these oracles. She is not the mother. As a matter of fact she is not part of the oracles at all.

(6) The sin of the mother is in having hired lovers. The hired lovers are Assyria and Egypt:

FIRST EDITION OF HOSEA 1 TO 3 ACCORDING TO GALE YEE
IN HER BOOK *Composition and Tradition in the Book of Hosea*

* VERSE NUMBERS FROM HEBREW BIBLE DO NOT CORRESPOND WITH ENGLISH R.S.V.

SUBTRACT 2 TO DETERMINE RSV VERSE NUMBERS.

HOSEA ☐

COLLECTOR ■

1	2	3
Beginning of Yahweh's speaking to Hosea v. 2	Plead with your mother 4aA*	In the first edition of Hosea's oracles the five verses of chapter three did not appear.
Hosea took Gomer v. 3	She is not my wife 4aB*	
	That she remove her harlotry 4b–5*	
First child (Jezreel) v. 4	Upon her children no pity 6–7a*	Chapter three did not appear as part of the book until the Exile.
Second child (Lo Rohama) v. 6	I will go after my lovers. 7b*	
	I will expose her 12*	The five verses of chapter three eventually separated the allegory from the rest of the book. This was the work of "ER."
Third child (Lo Ammi) v. 9	Call me "my husband" 18aBb*	
	I will betroth you to me 21–22a*	

> Ephraim is like a dove, silly and without sense,
>   calling to Egypt, going to Assyria (7:11).

> Israel is swallowed up;
>   already they are among the nations as a useless vessel.
> For they have gone up to Assyria,
>   a wild ass wandering alone;
> Ephraim has hired lovers.
> Though they hire allies among the nations,
>   I will soon gather them up (8:9–10).

The oracles of Hosea were preserved orally. Before we move to the first written edition of Hosea, I would suggest that you reread the above list of facts concerning the oracles of Hosea. With each written edition, the nature of the oracles will change. The content of the oracles will take on different meaning as each author and redactor adds introductions, conclusions, editorial comments, and, in some cases, insertions into the oracles themselves. These subsequent authors had the greatest respect for the edition they inherited (oral or otherwise). They were convinced of the great value of Hosea's oracles, and their sole purpose was to update his truth and apply it to a new situation, a crisis facing the nation, or an opportunity presenting itself.

THE COLLECTOR AND THE FIRST WRITTEN EDITION OF HOSEA

In the fourth year of King Hezekiah, which was the seventh year of Hoshea son of Elah, king of Israel, Shalmaneser king of Assyria came up against Samaria and besieged it. In the sixth year of Hezekiah, which was the ninth year of Hoshea king of Israel, Samaria was taken (2 Kgs 18:8–10).

Behind this bland description of Samaria's end were scenes of incredible cruelty. The destruction of a nation is horrible, and profound theological implications surface for generations following such a calamity.

Following the tragic events of 722–721 when the Assyrian army completely destroyed the city of Samaria and brought to an end the northern kingdom of Israel, former citizens of Samaria who were able to escape captivity fled south to Judah, taking with them their own characteristic religious beliefs. Not all of those who fled south were worshipers of Yahweh. Many had no desire to preserve anything more than their own skin. But we can believe without doubt that among those who escaped were to be found champions of Yahweh, persons whose faith, though changed, would continue and would even flourish as a result of their grief and loss. These would preserve important northern theological viewpoints. Refugees would become the seeds of the Deuteronomic reformation which would blossom a hundred years later and give birth to Judaism. And they would preserve the oracles of Hosea and oracles of other prophets whose names we do not know.

I think it is safe to assume that most of the escaped citizens of Samaria who fled to Judah ended up living in Jerusalem. These former urban dwellers would not compound the shock of radical change by choosing rural village life when they were already urbanized by nature. In Jerusalem they would exert influence on the future development of the cult of Yahweh.

But that's jumping ahead in our story. First we have to turn our attention to Hezekiah who reigned in Jerusalem shortly after the fall of Samaria (715–687). Dr. Yee suggested that at this time the collector produced the first written version of Hosea's oracles.[4] For a part of Hezekiah's reign there may have been hope of a reunion with some of the areas of the north. This tradition is preserved in Chronicles:

> So couriers went throughout all Israel and Judah with letters from the king and his princes, as the king had commanded, saying, O people of Israel, return to the Lord, the God of Abraham, Isaac, and Israel, that he may turn again to the remnant of you who have

escaped from the hand of the kings of Assyria. . . . So
the couriers went from city to city through the country
of Ephraim and Manasseh, and as far as Zebulun (2
Chr 30:5–10).

Now we reproduce the first three chapters of the *first* written
edition of the book of Hosea below. Please note that the words in
italics are the original oracles of Hosea:

When the Lord first spoke through Hosea, the Lord
said to Hosea, "Go take to yourself a wife of harlotry
and have children of harlotry, for the land commits
great harlotry by forsaking the Lord." So he went and
took Gomer the daughter of Diblaim and she conceived
and bore him a son.

And the Lord said to him, "Call his name Jezreel; for
yet a little while, and I will punish the house of Jehu for
the blood of Jezreel, and I will put an end to the kingdom of the house of Israel."

She conceived again and bore a daughter. And the
Lord said to him, "Call her name Not Pitied, for I will
no more have pity on the house of Israel, to forgive
them at all."

When she had weaned Not pitied, she conceived and
bore a son. And the Lord said, "Call his name Not my
people, for you are not my people and I am not your
God."

Plead with your mother, plead—
    for she is not my wife,
    and I am not her husband—
That she put away her harlotry from her face,
    and her adultery from between her breasts;
lest I strip her naked
    and make her as in the day she was born,
and make her like a wilderness,
    and set her like a parched land,
    and slay her with thirst.

Upon her children also I will have no pity,
    because they are children of harlotry.
For their mother has played the harlot;
    she that conceived them has acted shamefully.

For she said, "I will go after my lovers,
    who give me my bread and my water,
    my wool and my flax, my oil and my drink."

Now I will uncover her lewdness in the sight of her
        lovers,
    and no one shall rescue her out of my hand.

You will call me, "My Husband," and no longer will
you call me, "My Baal."

I will betroth you to me forever; I will betroth you to
me in righteousness and in justice, in steadfast love and
in mercy. I will betroth you to me in faithfulness.

(Hosea 1:2–4, 6, 8; 2:2–5, 10, 16, 19)

Earlier, after we identified the oracles of Hosea, we said that
Gomer had no place in these oracles. It was the first *written*
edition of Hosea, the work of the collector, which introduced
Gomer into the book and changed forever the original meaning
of the oracles.

Why did the collector mention the name of Gomer? For that
matter, why did he mention the name of Hosea? Before the collector wrote his book, popular tradition about the oracles provided the audience with information about them. If they were
recited for an audience (and truthfully we know little about how
this oral stage operated) the person reciting them would probably
tell the audience that these were the oracles of Hosea. If someone
asked "Who was Hosea?" answers were supplied from traditional
information.

One of the traditional pieces of information about Hosea,
Amos, Isaiah, and also Micah was that Yahweh had spoken to

DIVISION OF HOSEA 1 TO 3 ACCORDING TO GALE YEE
IN HER BOOK *Composition and Tradition in the Book of Hosea*

1	2	2	3
Title v. 1	Called sons of . . . God v. 1-3	I take back my grain 11	The Lord said to me (first person account) v. 1-3
Lord speaks to Hosea (3rd person) v. 2-4	Plead with your mother v. 4aA	No one shall rescue 12	Exile and return v. 4-5
Break bow of Israel v. 5	Not my wife v. 4aB	Lay waste her vines 13-15a	
Not pitied v. 6abA	Put away her harlotry 4b-5	Me, she forgot 15b-18aA	
Pity on Judah v. 6bB-7	Children of harlotry 6-7a	Call me my husband 18aBb	
Not my people v. 8-9	I will go after lovers 7b	Remove names of Baal 19-20	
	Erect wall against her 8-9	Betroth you forever 21-22a	
	I gave her wine and oil 10a	You shall know Yahweh 22b-25	
	Gold used for Baal 10b		

VERSE NUMBERS FROM
HEBREW BIBLE MAY
NOT CORRESPOND WITH
ENGLISH R.S.V.

HOSEA (white)
COLLECTOR (black)
R1 (grid)
R2 (hatched)

(Chart by Dr. William J. Doorly)

and through the prophet. Hosea was a true prophet. That's why the collector was writing down Hosea's oracles. The collector was living in an environment, a time and place, which encouraged the production and use of written documents. We said that the place was Jerusalem, and the time was the reign of Hezekiah. The collector started quite naturally with the words, "When the Lord first spoke through Hosea . . ."

It is popular to say that the collector was a disciple of Hosea, but we know very little about the disciples of the eighth century prophets if they had disciples. The collector may have been a priest, a Levite. It is safe to say that he was a forerunner of the Deuteronomists of Josiah's day. But this was sixty years before Josiah.

GOMER

I do not think it is necessary to believe that Gomer was a harlot. Gomer is only mentioned one time in the book of Hosea. This is a fact which many students choose to ignore. It is *possible* that the sentence which identifies her as a woman of harlotry means only that she was an Israelite. The oracles of Hosea identify Israel as a harlot, and the people as practitioners of harlotry. With this in mind the collector may have been saying that Hosea married a woman of Israel (already destroyed at the time the collector wrote his book) and that Hosea was right in calling Israel a people of harlotry. Gomer was one of those people.

What about the names of the children? These names are obviously symbolic. The names may be part of an allegory to portray the teachings of Hosea. The "children" may be another name for the teachings of Hosea. If this were true, and it is only a speculation, then maybe there was no wife named Gomer. Perhaps Gomer was a symbolic name also, the meaning of which is lost to us.

This line of thought is not outside the possibility of reason. According to our identification of Hosea's oracles, *he never mentions his wife Gomer by name.*

Another approach would be to suppose that the collector was familiar with the marriage of Hosea, and that this marriage had been less than ideal. It may have been a troubled marriage. The collector, looking back on the teachings of Hosea concerning the relationship between Yahweh and Israel (Ephraim), reached the conclusion that Hosea gained insight into this unsatisfactory relationship because of his own unsatisfactory relationship with his wife.[5]

We stated earlier that the "mother" referred to in the legal complaint which the children are urged to bring by Hosea, "Plead with your mother, plead—" is Israel, Samaria, or Rachel, the favorite wife of Jacob, who appears as a counter-hero (a deceiver) in the conclusion of the book. Jacob, whose name was changed to Israel, was the father of the Israelites. Remember the words of Deuteronomy, "A wandering Aramean was my father." In the original oracles of Hosea *the mother was not Gomer, and the children were not her children.* The children were the children of Israel.

Whatever the intentions of the collector, by his introduction to the oracles the players were forever changed. The mother became Gomer in the eyes of the reader, and the children became her children. I do not believe that the collector intended for the reader to reach this conclusion. Literally this would not be consistent. The children of Gomer have symbolic names. The collector used these names to portray what he knew, and his readers knew, had happened to Israel in the tragic events of 722/721. As I see it, the names of the children of Gomer were important, not the children themselves.

THE COLLECTOR'S TASK

The collector took the oracles of Hosea and gave them an introduction. It is possible that he arranged them in the order in which they appear now in the book. He first provided an introduction, and in the introduction, Dr. Yee points out, he legitimized the oracles of Hosea by declaring that Yahweh spoke to Hosea (1:2). By legitimizing Hosea's oracles, he also legitimized his own written document. Yee writes:

> The collector, furthermore, legitimates himself and the collection which he creates. He lacked the call from

God and the deeds of power which seemed to support a prophetic ministry. However he carries on the prophet's work by compiling and assembling the sayings into a literary tradition. . . . We tentatively date the collector after the fall of the northern kingdom in 722/21 BCE. Sentiments of hope could have sprung up during the time of Hezekiah's reform (715–705?). During this time Hezekiah had approached the citizen's of the defunct North to participate in the reform program. It was anticipated that religious unification between North and South would serve as a prelude to political unification.[6]

The oracle chosen to be first in the collection was one which used language of a legal suit brought against someone called the mother. The mother was the harlotrous Israel. (Dr. Yee says that the mother was originally Rachel, the matriarch of Ephraim/Benjamin.) The purpose of the legal suit was to get the mother to stop her harlotry, and the punishment was to be stripped in public and humiliated. It was not a divorce proceeding. The collector, however, perhaps with the destruction of Israel in mind, turned it into a divorce proceeding by introducing the words:

> for she is not my wife,
> and I am not her husband.

The collector, building on the oracles of Hosea, envisioned the relationship between Israel and Yahweh as a marriage relationship. Because Israel was destroyed, he introduced the divorce theme. The relationship was broken, destroyed, because the wife played the harlot.

The sin which Hosea condemned was the complete reliance on military strength and, consequently, foreign alliances, for survival, instead of relying on the ancient alliance with Yahweh. Hosea was a conservative champion of Yahweh. The relationship with Yahweh which Israel had in its past was the relationship which Hosea believed that the leaders of Israel had destroyed.

They turned to Egypt for protection against Assyria, and to Assyria for protection against Egypt.

> Ephraim is like a dove, silly and without sense,
>   calling to Egypt, going to Assyria (7:11).

> Israel is swallowed up;
>   already they are among the nations as a useless vessel.
> For they have gone up to Assyria,
>   a wild ass wandering alone;
>   Ephraim has hired lovers.
> Though they hire allies among the nations,
>   I will soon gather them up (8:9–10).

The collector who produced the first written version of Hosea's oracles did not introduce the view that the sins of Israel were primarily related to the practice of false religion, namely Baalism. This view was introduced into the book of Hosea one hundred years after Hosea's death in the days of King Josiah by a zealous levitical scribe whom we will call the Josianic redactor. This scribe incorporated his polemical material concerning Israel and Baalism into the book of Hosea because he believed it was in the best interest of Judah and his audience. He may have believed that Hosea had condemned Baalism by inference, and thus the Josianic redactor may have felt it was his responsibility to make this more evident.

Before we turn to this redactor and his concerns, we will summarize the work of the collector.

(a) Producing the first written edition of Hosea's oracles, the collector selected the oracles of Hosea to be included, and arranged them in order.

(b) The collector introduced Gomer into the book. He may have introduced Gomer to give information about her three children who have symbolic names. The symbolic names of the children of Hosea have reference to the fate of the nation in view of the tragic events of 722.

Whatever the collector's intention, the mother of the lawsuit in chapter 2, who was originally Rachel, the favorite wife of Jacob (or Samaria, or Israel), ended up being identified by readers as Gomer. In the original oracles of Hosea, Gomer played no role.

(c) The collector introduced the words "she is not my wife and I am not her husband." This changed the lawsuit, demanding that the wife change her behavior and "put away her harlotry," into a divorce proceeding. The divorce is symbolic of the fact that Israel the nation had been destroyed in the collector's past. Hosea had not written of a divorce. The collector was reinterpreting the oracle of Hosea to suit changed conditions.

(d) Dr. Yee says that the hope for a remarriage (a rebetrothal) is introduced by the collector. Yee writes:

> Contrary to scholars like Marti and Harper who consign all hope passages to the exilic period, the message of hope is introduced by the northern tradent who first assembled the tradition.[7]

THE JOSIANIC REDACTOR

In the days of Josiah, the little kingdom of Judah was virtually free of Assyrian domination. Josiah was able to capitalize on Assyria's weakness. In the early reign of Josiah there was great optimism concerning the reestablishment of Israel as it had been in the days of David. Judah planned to annex the land to its north which had formerly belonged to the kingdom of Israel.

At this time the Deuteronomistic movement became the motivator of the military, political, and economic movement toward the recapture of Israel's old glory. To support this goal the Deuteronomists decided to centralize all religious activity in the temple at Jerusalem. All religious practices would conform to the ideals of Deuteronomistic theology. The Deuteronomists were zealous champions of Yahweh. In order to strengthen and control the exclusive worship of Yahweh, all Assyrian and Canaanite religious practices were forbidden, and worship at high places and shrines throughout Judah and in nearby Israel were to come to an end.

In these days there was a great amount of scribal activity. The zealous levitical circle of priests and scribes (whom we call the Deuteronomists) produced the first edition of the master-piece which we call the Deuteronomistic History. It was a theological history, the first edition of which was written to demonstrate why Israel was destroyed and what Judah had to do to survive. This activity was supported by the amazing discovery of the torah of Yahweh in the temple while the temple was being cleaned and repaired. In the Deuteronomistic History the discovery of the torah is said to have initiated the reforms of Josiah. In the second book of Chronicles the reforms of Josiah are said to have been underway for many years before the discovery of the torah.[8]

In the Josianic age the scribes of the Deuteronomists also produced updated versions of the four eighth century prophets, including the book of Hosea. The scribes embraced the values of the oracles of the eighth century prophets, appropriated their teachings and produced new editions addressed to problems of their age.

In section I of Hosea (chapters 1 to 3) these are the words which Dr. Yee identifies as those added to produce the Josianic edition of the book of Hosea. They constitute a commentary on the fall of the northern kingdom:

> And she did not know
> > that it was I who gave her
> > the grain, the wine, and the oil. . . .
> Therefore I will take back
> > my grain in its time,
> > and my wine in its season;
> And I will take away my wool and my flax,
> > which were to cover her nakedness. . . .
> And I will put an end to all her mirth,
> > her feasts, her new moons, her sabbaths,
> > and all her appointed feasts.
> And I will lay waste her vines and her fig trees,
> > of which she said,
> "These are my hire,
> > which my lovers have given me."
> I will make them a forest,

and the beasts of the field shall devour them.
And I will punish her for the feast days of the Baals
   when she burned incense to them
And decked herself with her ring and jewelry,
   and went after her lovers (2:8–9, 11–13).

The first thing we notice about this added commentary is its relation to some Deuteronomistic words and concepts. In the torah of the Deuteronomist the tithe is composed of a portion of "your grain or of your wine or of your oil" (Deuteronomy 12:17 and 14:23). This author says of Israel:

And she did not know
   that it was I who gave her
   the grain, the wine, and the oil (2:8).

Further, the mention of burning incense is singled out significantly in the Deuteronomistic History. The most striking example is in a prophecy concerning the future activity of the king in whose reign this expansion of Hosea was made.

Behold a son shall be born to the house of David, Josiah
by name: and he shall sacrifice upon you the priests of
the high places who burn incense upon you, and men's
bones shall be burned upon you (1 Kgs 13:3).

The Josianic redactor of the book of Hosea builds on the metaphor of the wife but introduces a new interpretation of her sin by redefining her lovers. In the oracles of Hosea we said that Israel's lovers were foreign political powers (Assyria and Egypt) with which the political leaders of Samaria made alliances for their survival, rejecting an ancient pact made between Yahweh and Israel. In the eyes of Hosea these alliances constituted *the rejection of Yahweh* and the destruction of the relationship between the nation and her faithful savior of earlier times.

The Josianic redactor agrees entirely with Hosea that the sin of Israel is the rejection of Yahweh, but he is not interested in accusing Israel, long gone at the time of his redaction, of unsound political decisions. His main interest is in attacking *corrupt religious practices* referred to frequently in the Deuteronomistic History as the sins of Jeroboam. Yahweh says, "I will put an end to all her mirth, her feasts, her new moons, her sabbaths, and all her appointed feasts" (2:11). In particular the sins attacked are associated with the altar at Bethel.

> And Jeroboam appointed a feast on the fifteenth day of the eighth month like the feast that was in Judah, and he offered sacrifices upon the altar; so he did in Bethel, sacrificing to the calves that he had made. And he placed in Bethel the priests of the high places that he had made. He went up to the altar which he had made on the fifteenth day in the eighth month, in the month he had devised of in his heart; and he ordained a feast for the people of Israel, and went to the altar to burn incense (1 Kgs 12:32–33).

It is this altar at Bethel which King Josiah completely destroyed and then further defiled by burning the bones of corpses on its stones (2 Kgs 23:15–16).

We will be able to develop this viewpoint to a greater extent when we move to sections II and III (chapters 4 to 14) of the book of Hosea. For the time being we should note that the Josianic editor is concerned primarily in promoting cultic purity which he identifies as worshiping Yahweh in the one place where Yahweh has chosen to place his name. In Jerusalem, under the control of Deuteronomist priests and scribes, all Assyrian and Canaanite religious practices will be eliminated, and the cult of Yahweh will be perfect. He writes at a time when Josiah was still alive.

Now here is an important observation concerning the words of the Josianic redactor: What Israel is he speaking of? He is speaking of the former northern kingdom. Since that is the case, he does not have to introduce the concept of returning to Yahweh, either as a concept or as an exhortation. Because the Israel of which he wrote was gone, returning to Yahweh was out of the question. This editor is interested in Israel's behavior as a lesson for his fellow Judeans. The theme of returning to Yahweh, which is a very important, key Deuteronomistic theme, would not enter the picture until after the death of Josiah and the destruction of Jerusalem. In the exilic period the important religious concept of repentance emerged.

THE EXILIC REDACTOR

The final edition of the book of Hosea, the canonical book, was the effort of an exilic redactor. He was responsible for some of the most profound themes in Hosea. We will discuss in detail the work of this scribe in a later chapter devoted to his work and theology.

To conclude this review of the growth and development of section I (chapters 1 to 3) of Hosea we will note a few logistical facts.

It was the final author who divided the book into three sections by bracketing each section. He is responsible for beginning each section with an accusation (1:2, 4:1, 12:1–2) and ending each section with Yahweh's people returning (3:5, 11:11, 14:7).

He opens the book by writing:

> The word of Yahweh that came to Hosea the son of Beeri, in the days of Uzziah, Jotham, Ahaz, and Hezekiah, kings of Judah, and in the days of Jeroboam the son of Joash, king of Israel (1:1).

Because this author was a Judean he mentions the Judean kings first. His thoughts are with Judah. In chapter 3 when he speaks of Israel, he is speaking of Judeans in exile whom he calls the children of Israel. As we suggested earlier in Chapter II, during the exile the name Israel came to mean all the people of Yahweh. In fact, for this author, the people of Israel, even those whose ancestors were refugees from the north, were now Judeans, many of them in exile, but all of them emerging from a long period of intense suffering. He is a healer. He shares many optimistic theological perceptions with the author of Deutero-Isaiah. He declares that Yahweh "will have pity on the house of

Judah," changing the name of Not Pitied. It is he who writes in response to the name of the third child, Not my people:

> Yet the number of the people of Israel shall be like the sand of the sea, which can be neither measured nor numbered; and in the place where it was said to them, "You are not my people," it shall be said to them, "Sons of the Living Gods." And the people of Israel shall be gathered together, and they shall appoint for themselves one head; and they shall go up from the land, for great shall be the day of Jezreel (1:10–11).

The exilic redactor ends section I of Hosea by inserting five verses which now constitute the third chapter. By his insertion he concluded the allegory of the bad marriage and separated the allegory from the rest of the collection of Hosea's oracles.

SUMMARY AND CONCLUSION OF SECTION I

The section we have been discussing, chapters 1 to 3, like the rest of the book of Hosea reached its final form in several steps during a period spanning two hundred years. In the oracles of Hosea the figure of the mother started as a simple metaphor for Israel (or perhaps Rachel as the eponymous mother of Israel, as Dr. Yee suggests). Hosea had no intention of constructing an allegory.

The activity of Israel which provoked the charge of unfaithfulness and harlotry from Hosea was described by him with these words:

> Ephraim has hired lovers (8:9).

The sin of Israel was the rejection of Yahweh in the form of the destruction of an ancient dependent relationship on Yahweh for survival and the substitution of foreign political alliances in place of this relationship of trust. *This was the sin of Israel against which Hosea railed.* There is nothing in the oracles of

Hosea about Baalism or participation of Israelites in fertility ri of Canaan.

When the oracles of Hosea were first put into written for the first editor, the collector, provided the wife of Hosea and t three children with symbolic names. A simple metaphor ol wife/mother turned into an allegory at that point. For better worse, from this time forward the wife/mother would have double identity as Israel/Gomer.

The collector made another vital change to the mater which he inherited. He changed a legal proceeding (obscu though it is) against a wife, taken to force her to behave like a w and fulfill her filial obligations, into a divorce proceeding. V suggested that this interpretive projection into the older mater resulted from the collector's belief that the tragic events of 7 were better pictured as a divorce of Israel by Yahweh. So added the words:

> . . . she is not my wife,
> and I am not her husband (2:2).

If, in the collector's mind, Israel was the unfaithful wife, after h destruction she could not be disciplined to behave like a go wife, legal proceeding or otherwise. This does not mean that t collector was completely pessimistic about Israel. According Dr. Yee, the rebetrothal of Israel and Yahweh (2:19) may be hope of the collector who lived in Judah in the days of Hezekia

> Hezekiah sent to all Israel and Judah, and wrote letters
> also to Ephraim and Manasseh, that they should come
> to the house of the Lord at Jerusalem (2 Chr 30:1).

The second written edition of Hosea appeared near the ei of the seventh century during the reign of Josiah as part of a explosion of scribal activity of the zealous Deuteronomic circ The Deuteronomistic scribes who expanded the collector's ec tion of Hosea saw the obvious great value of Hosea's eighth ce tury oracles and reinterpreted their truth in forms particulai applicable and valuable for addressing seventh century probler and concerns. The Deuteronomists were not willing to interpret the sin of Israel simply as political alliances with foreign powers. Scribal activity expanded the interpretation of the sin of rejection of Yahweh to include participation in many forms of Canaanite and Assyrian religious rites which did not conform to the Deuteronomistic concepts of cultic purity. We will discuss this period in Chapter VIII, "The Josianic Edition of the Book of Hosea."

The final edition of Hosea appeared one hundred years later, near the end of the exilic period. This author/editor whom we call the exilic redactor determined the final structure of the book and introduced the concept of repentance in conjunction with the later Deuteronomistic concept of returning to Yahweh and returning to the land (3:5). His contribution to the allegory includes the reversal of the names of the three children.

THE FINAL STATE OF THE ALLEGORY

What started out as a simple metaphor grew into an allegory as the result of the expansions of three redactors. This is not the recommended way to construct an allegory. A work of literary art is seldom produced by a committee, especially when its members live decades, even centuries apart, and have different purposes and viewpoints.

Nevertheless I believe there is something magnificent about the first three chapters of Hosea. To appreciate the power and beauty of this unit we have to put forth an effort to suspend our demand for linear logic. The ancient Israelites were simply not aware of a need for logic. If we are able to alter our approach to these passages we will recognize a mixture of poetry and prose which is capable of producing a unique impact on the reader. As we suggested in Chapter IV, think of the book of Hosea as a musical score, with section I as the overture. Several themes are introduced, sometimes contrasting with each other, as is common in great music. No theme in the overture is over-developed. Together the themes form an artistic unity providing a base for that which follows. The overture prepares the audience, the listeners (the readers), for the power of the composition which follows.

PART TWO

CHAPTER VI

The Oracles of Hosea

Plead with your mother, plead—
That she put away her harlotry from her face,
*   and her adultery from between her breasts;*
lest I strip her naked
*   and make her as in the day she was born,*
and make her like a wilderness,
*   and set her like a parched land,*
*   and slay her with thirst.*

For she said, "I will go after my lovers,
*   who give me my bread and my water,*
*   my wool and my flax, my oil and my drink."*

Now I will uncover her lewdness
*   in the sight of her lovers,*
*   and no one shall rescue her out of my hand.*

[Complete oracles of Hosea in Chapters 1 through 3.]

The platform upon which the eighth century prophets built their oracles was very narrow. If we read the *final* version of these prophetic books, the canonical versions, and fail to understand that the original oracles provided little more than the core of the book, and that several subsequent authors expanded the earlier editions, we will reach fictitious and misleading conclusions concerning the original prophets.

The eighth century prophets Amos and Hosea were intensely concerned with only one or two of the theological issues which later filled the books which now bear their names.

In order to appreciate fully the clarity and intensity of the original oracles, we have to read them and analyze them apart from the editorial and redactional accretions of later editions. Below we will reproduce, more or less, the original oracles of Hosea (chapters 4–14) as identified by Dr. Gale Yee in her book *Composition and Tradition in the Book of Hosea: A Redactional Critical Investigation.*

It will assist us greatly in reading these oracles if we remember the audience for which they were intended. Hosea (and Amos also incidently) did not address his oracles to the people of Israel at large. *The masses are not addressed.* The eighth century oracles of Hosea were primarily directed to a particular audience, the powerful elite of Samaria, the king and his advisors, including a circle of priests, generals, and court prophets. If we keep this in mind it will assist us in our movement toward understanding Hosea's concerns. His concerns are political concerns.

> Yet let no one contend
>   and let none accuse,
>   for with you is my contention
>   and I will destroy your mother.

> For a spirit of harlotry has led them astray.

> Hear this, O priests!
>   Give heed, O house of Israel!
> Hearken, O house of the King!
>   For the judgment pertains to you;
> for you have been a snare at Mizpah,
>   and a net spread upon Tabor.
> And they have made a deep pit of Shittim.

> I know Ephraim,
>   and Israel is not hid from me;
> for now, O Ephraim, you have played the harlot,
>   Israel is defiled.
> The pride of Ephraim testifies to his face;
>   Ephraim shall stumble in his guilt;

Blow the horn in Gibeah, the trumpet in Ramah.
  Sound the alarm in Beth-aven; tremble, O Benjamin!
Ephraim shall become a desolation in the day of
    punishment;
  among the tribes of Israel I declare what is sure.
The princes of Judah have become like those who remove
    the landmark;
  upon whom I will pour out my wrath like water.
Ephraim is oppressed, crushed in judgment,
  because he was determined to go after vanity.
Therefore I am like a moth to Ephraim,
  and like dry rot to the house of Judah.

When Ephraim saw his sickness, and Judah his wound,
  then Ephraim went to Assyria, and sent to the great King.

For I will be like a lion to Ephraim,
  and like a young lion to the house of Judah.
I, even I, will rend and go away,
  I will carry off, and none shall escape.

Gilead is a city of evildoers,
  tracked with blood.
As robbers lie in wait for a man,
  so the priests are banded together;
they murder on the way to Shechem,
  yea, they commit villainy.
In the house of Israel I have seen a horrible thing;
  Ephraim's harlotry is there, Israel is defiled.
the corruption of Ephraim is revealed,
  and the wicked deeds of Samaria;
for they deal falsely, the thief breaks in,
  and the bandits raid without
But they do not consider
  that I remember all their evil works.
Now their deeds encompass them,
  they are before my face.

By their wickedness they make the king glad,
   and the princes by their treachery.

On the day of our king the princes
   became sick with the heat of wine;
     he stretched out his hand with mockers.
For like an oven their hearts burn with intrigue;
   all night their anger smolders;
     in the morning it blazes like a flaming fire.
All of them are hot as an oven,
   and they devour their rulers.
All their kings have fallen;
   and none of them calls upon me.

Ephraim is like a dove, silly and without sense,
   calling to Egypt, going to Assyria.
As they go, I will spread over them my net;
   I will bring them down like birds of the air;

Woe to them, for they have strayed from me!
Destruction to them, for they have rebelled against me!
I would redeem them, but they speak lies against me.

They do not cry to me from the heart,
   but they wail upon their beds;
     for grain and wine they gash themselves. . . .
Although I trained and strengthened their arms,
   yet they devise evil against me.

Israel is swallowed up;
   already they are among the nations as a useless vessel.
For they have gone up to Assyria, a wild ass wandering
     alone;
   Ephraim has hired lovers.
Though they hire allies among the nations,
   I will soon gather them up.
And they shall cease for a little while
   from anointing king and princes.

Ephraim's glory shall fly away like a bird—
    no birth, no pregnancy, no conception!
Even if they bring up children,
    I will bereave them till none is left.
    Woe to them when I depart from them!
Ephraim's sons, as I have seen, are determined for a prey;
    Ephraim must lead forth his sons to slaughter.

Ephraim is stricken, their root dried up,
    they shall bear no fruit.
Even though they bring forth,
    I will slay their beloved children.

Ephraim was a trained heifer that loved to thresh,
    and I spared her fair neck;
but I will put Ephraim to the yoke, Judah must plow,
    Jacob must harrow for himself.

You have plowed iniquity, you have reaped injustice,
    you have eaten the fruit of lies.
Ephraim has encompassed me with lies,
    and the house of Israel with deceit;

Ephraim herds the wind,
    and pursues the east wind all day long;
they multiply falsehood and violence;
    they make a bargain with Assyria,
    and oil is carried to Egypt.

The Lord has an indictment against Judah,
    and will punish Jacob according to his deeds.
In the womb he took his brother by the heel,
    and in his manhood he strove with God.

A trader, in whose hands are false balances,
    he loves to oppress.
Ephraim has said, "Ah, but I am rich,
    I have gained wealth for myself";

(Jacob fled to the land of Aram,
   there Israel did service for a wife,
   and for a wife he herded sheep.)

The iniquity of Ephraim is bound up,
   his sin is kept in store.
The pangs of childbirth come for him,
   but he is an unwise son;
for now he does not present himself
   at the mouth of the womb.

Though he may flourish as the reed plant,
   the east wind, the wind of the Lord, shall come,
   rising from the wilderness;
and his fountain shall dry up,
   his spring shall be parched;
   it shall strip his treasury of every precious thing.
Samaria shall bear her guilt,
   because she has rebelled against her God;
they shall fall by the sword,
   their little ones shall be dashed in pieces,
   and their pregnant women ripped open.

THE AUDIENCE OF HOSEA

Hosea, like Amos, did not deliver a general message to a general audience of hearers. It is vital to our understanding of Hosea that we understand that he is directing his oracles to a specific audience in the capital city of Samaria. After the opening oracle (where Hosea may be theoretically speaking to the masses) he is speaking to the powerful rulers of Israel, the king and his advisors, generals, priests, and court prophets.

Hear this, O priests!
   Give heed, O house of Israel!
Hearken, O house of the king!
   For the judgment pertains to you (5:1–2).

It is in conjunction with the correct identification of Hosea's audience that the sin of Israel, against which Hosea speaks, is properly identified. It is only the powerful decision makers of Israel, the nation's political leaders, who are able to make alliances with foreign nations for protection against potential enemies. It is in the making of these foreign alliances that Israel has played the harlot.

For a spirit of harlotry has led them astray (4:12).

O Ephraim, you have played the harlot (5:3).

. . . the corruption of Ephraim is revealed,
and the wicked deeds of Samaria (7:1).

Ephraim is like a dove, silly and without sense,
calling to Egypt, going to Assyria (7:11).

Israel is swallowed up;
already they are among the nations as a useless vessel.
For they have gone up to Assyria,
a wild ass wandering alone;
Ephraim has hired lovers.
Though they hire allies among the nations,
I will soon gather them up (8:8–10).

THE HISTORICAL BACKGROUND OF THE EIGHTH CENTURY ORACLES

If the oracles of Hosea are chiefly directed to the decision makers of Samaria, then it is necessary for us to familiarize ourselves with the violent and tumultuous behavior of these leaders during the time of Hosea's prophetic activity. Familiarity will make it possible for us to appreciate the judgmental rage which permeates these oracles. Here are the violent facts.

It is known that the days of Jeroboam II (784–753) were days of peace and prosperity, partly because Assyria was distracted and preoccupied with other problems. This peace ended when a usurper of the Assyrian throne came to power giving himself the name of a previous Assyrian king, Tiglath-pileser III. In the thirty-one year period from the death of Jeroboam II to the tragic events of 722 there were six kings on the throne of Israel. (See our chart entitled "Chronology of the Last Days of Israel." In the twelve year period following the death of Jeroboam, three of the four kings took the throne by murdering their predecessor.)

The son of Jeroboam II, Zechariah, was assassinated by Shallum after reigning for only six months.

> Shallum . . . conspired against him [Zechariah], and struck him down at Ibleam, and killed him, and reigned in his stead (2 Kgs 15:10).

The assassin of Zechariah, Shallum, was killed by Menahem after a one month reign. Menahem became a vassal of Tiglath-pileser, whose name in Babylon was Pul.

> Pul the king of Assyria came against the land; and Menahem gave Pul a thousand talents of silver, that he might help him to confirm his hold of the royal power. Menahem exacted the money from Israel, that is, from all the wealthy men, fifty shekels of silver from every man, to give to the king of Assyria (2 Kgs 15:19–20).

Menahem, who put this burden of taxation on Israel for protection of the Assyrian king, reigned for ten years. His son Pekahiah reigned for two years and was killed by Pekah who reigned in his stead. Pekah allied with Rezin of Syria and marched against Ahaz of Judah. This is known as the Syro-Ephraimite war, and led to ugly consequences for Judah.

> So Ahaz sent messengers to Tiglath-pileser king of Assyria, saying, "I am your servant and your son. Come

CHRONOLOGY OF THE
LAST DAYS OF ISRAEL

KING OF ISRAEL	APPROX- IMATE DATES	COMMENTS
JEROBOAM II	784–753	Israel enjoyed peace and prosperity while Assyria was distracted and preoccupied.
ZECHARIAH	753–752	Killed by Shallum after reigning for only six months. This was the end of the house of Jehu.
SHALLUM	752	Killed by Menahem after one month.
MENAHEM	752–742	Paid a large tribute of one thousand talents of silver to the Assyrian king Tiglath-pileser, also called Pul.
PEKAHIAH	742–741	Killed by Pekah after two years.
PEKAH	741–730	With Rezin, king of Syria, he went to war against Ahaz of Judah (Syro-Ephraimite war). Ahaz called on Tiglath-pileser for help. Ahaz eventually sent silver and gold from the temple to the king of Assyria.
HOSHEA	730–722/1	He early became a vassal of king Shalmaneser and paid tribute. Later he stopped paying tribute and looked to Egypt for help. After three years of siege the city of Samaria was completely destroyed by the Assyrians.

up, and rescue me from the hand of the king of Syria and from the hand of the king of Israel (Pekah), who are attacking me." Ahaz also took the silver and the gold that was found in the house of the Lord and in the treasures of the king's house, and sent a present to the king of Assyria (2 Kgs 16:7–8).

When Ahaz called himself a "son" of Tiglath-pileser, he was declaring himself to be a vassal. During the reign of Ahaz, Isaiah the eighth century prophet delivered oracles as a champion of Yahweh in Jerusalem.

During the reign of Pekah, the king of Israel (741–730), Assyria punished Israel for the activity of the Syro-Ephraimite war by ravaging the northern territories of Galilee and greatly reducing the borders of Israel. Shortly thereafter Pekah was slain and Hoshea began his reign in Samaria as a puppet of the successor of Tiglath-pileser, Shalmaneser V.

Hoshea was the last king of Israel (730–721). At first he was an Assyrian vassal, but Hoshea tried to form an alliance with Egypt against Assyria.

... the king of Assyria found treachery in Hoshea; for he had sent messengers to So, king of Egypt, and offered no tribute to the king of Assyria, as he had done year by year; therefore the king of Assyria shut him up, and bound him in prison. ... In the ninth year of Hoshea the king of Assyria captured Samaria, and he carried the Israelites away to Assyria (2 Kgs 17:4, 6).

The historical facts of the last days of the northern kingdom reveal tragic times for Israel, and as you read the chronicle of mayhem and bloodshed you get the clear impression that the ancient God of Israel, Yahweh, was abandoned by the so-called "powerful" of Samaria. Admittedly our main source of information for this time period is the Deuteronomistic History. There is not a hint in the account of the last thirty-one years of any acknowledgement of Yahweh's role in the history of the nation by any king, prince, or significant political leader. For the powerful of Samaria the ancient relationship between Israel and Yahweh was less than a memory.

THE WORSHIPERS OF YAHWEH IN THE LAST DAYS OF ISRAEL

If there were no champions of Yahweh in the royal court, there were some who remembered Yahweh in other places. They may have been few in number. Supporting this view that the worshipers of Yahweh were in the minority is a tradition of Elijah the Tishbite, an earlier northern prophet. After the contest between Elijah and the Tyrian prophets of Baal, Elijah is said to have complained to Yahweh in isolation at Horeb:

> . . . the people of Israel have forsaken thy covenant, thrown down thy altars, and slain thy prophets with the sword; and I, even I only, am left (1 Kgs 19:10).

I suggest that this tradition may be a reflection of the weakness and small number of the followers of Yahweh in Israel at various times in Israel's history. Regardless, there were champions of Yahweh during the last days of Israel, and Hosea ben Beeri was among their number. It would be helpful if we knew where the home of Hosea was, as we know the home of the three other eighth century prophets, Amos, Isaiah, and Micah. Unfortunately that information is not available for us. One of the differences between Israel and Judah is that in Israel the capital city, Samaria, was not the location of the state sanctuary. The major shrine for Israel was Bethel, located on the southern border, not more than fifteen miles from Jerusalem. The history of Bethel as a Yahwistic holy place and its location near Jerusalem made it a target of the Deuteronomists a hundred years after the death of Hosea. We will say more about that in Chapter VIII. Other important centers of Yahwistic worship included Shiloh and Shechem. When Jeroboam I first became king of Israel it is reported that he erected calves at two official national shrines, Dan and Bethel. Because of the distance of Dan from Jerusalem we hear nothing whatever about this shrine.

THE ORACLES OF HOSEA AND THE POLITICAL SITUATION OF ISRAEL

It hardly needs to be said that the oracles of Hosea are full of pain and anger. He saw Israel's leaders making all the wrong decisions and leading the people to economic and military destruction. Instead of calling on the ancient, long-standing relationship between Israel and Yahweh, Israel trusted in military strength for deliverance, either its own or the military strength of others. In running to these foreign powers Israel acted like a harlot.

> For she said, "I will go after my lovers,
>> who give me my bread and my water,
>> my wool and my flax, my oil and my drink" (2:5).

> I know Ephraim,
>> and Israel is not hid from me;
> for now, O Ephraim, you have played the harlot,
>> Israel is defiled (5:3).

There are some commentators who see references to specific political activity in some of Hosea's oracles—for example:

> On the day of our king the princes
>> became sick with the heat of wine;
>> he stretched out his hand with mockers.
> For like an oven their hearts burn with intrigue;
>> all night their anger smolders;
>> in the morning it blazes like a flaming fire.
> All of them are hot as an oven,
>> and they devour their rulers.
> All their kings have fallen;
>> and none of them calls upon me (7:5–7).

This oracle may refer to the assassination of Pekah who was replaced by Hoshea (2 Kgs 15:30), but we cannot be sure. In the twelve year period ending in 733 four kings were the victims of assassination.

The book of Hosea, like the other eighth century prophetic books, contains geographical references which are obscure to us, although they were not obscure to the original audience—references such as:

> . . . for you have been a snare at Mizpah,
>   and a net spread upon Tabor.
> And they have made deep the pit of Shittim (5:1–2).

> Gilead is a city of evildoers,
>   tracked with blood (6:8).

Regardless of the obscurity of these references to us, the feeling behind these oracles comes across loud and clear. There is no hiding the distress and pain of Hosea and the judgmental rage of Yahweh. For our purposes it is sufficient to note that the background for most of the oracles of Hosea was the period of the Syro-Ephraimite war. This background accounts for the several references to Judah in the eighth century oracles of Hosea (5:10, 14; 10:11; 12:2). The destructive activity of the Samarian power structure to which Hosea objected was mirrored in Jerusalem throughout the period in question.

THE USE OF METAPHOR BY HOSEA

Hosea had an inclination to use metaphor and metaphor-like comparison to increase the impact of his message and to express his feelings about Israel/Ephraim. There are probably more metaphors in the book of Hosea than any other fourteen chapters of Hebrew scripture. The eighth century prophet used metaphor liberally and is responsible for a dozen of the nearly thirty which are used to describe Israel in the canonical book. See our chart "Metaphors in Hosea for Israel/Ephraim by Author." The metaphors used by Hosea are all negative. Israel is a harlot, a silly dove, a useless vessel, a wild ass, a dishonest merchant. In a later chapter we will note a different feeling in the metaphors used to describe Israel by an unnamed exilic redactor. By making this distinction a reader of Hosea will gain a better understanding of the content and meaning of the eighth century oracles.

There are also metaphors for Yahweh in the book of Hosea, although not as many as there are for Israel (about a dozen). The only two metaphors for Yahweh which we can attribute with assurance to Hosea are both judgmental.

> For I will be like a lion to Ephraim,
> and like a young lion to the house of Judah (5:14).

> Therefore I am like a moth to Ephraim,
> and like dry rot to the house of Judah (5:12).

HOSEA AND THE CONCEPT OF COVENANT

It is stated in many commentaries that Hosea was angry and dispirited because Israel the nation had abandoned its ancient covenant (Hebrew, *berit,* or *berith*) with Yahweh. I object to this interpretation. The word "covenant" carries a weight of structure which I think was foreign to the feelings of Hosea. To begin with, the word "covenant" appears five times in the book of Hosea (2:18, 6:7, 8:1, 10:4, 12:1), but only once can it be identified as a part of an oracle of the eighth century prophet.

> . . . they multiply falsehood and violence;
> they make a bargain (*berit*) with Assyria,
> and oil is carried to Egypt (12:1).

A hundred years after the death of Hosea, the word "covenant" became popular as a description of a legal, structured relationship resembling the vassal treaty relationship between a superior military power (Assyria, for example) and a smaller weaker nation (such as Syria or Israel). The vassal relationship was seen to be of benefit to both parties. The subservient vassal of the stronger party would become a "protectorate." The covenant relationship had a number of clauses and conditions.[1]

This concept of "covenant" was adopted by legalistic theologians of Jerusalem in the late seventh century to describe an ancient relationship between Israel and Judah. They projected their concept of covenant into Israel's ancient past.

In the days of Hosea and Amos, this stiff definition of covenant was not current. Hosea was not angry because of the breaking of a contract. He was angry because the leaders of his nation had abandoned and rejected Yahweh in favor of military strength and alliances with strange political powers, thus destroying an ancient, living relationship with the God of Israel's youth. They had forgotten Yahweh. Yahweh didn't deserve that treatment.

HOSEA'S USE OF A JACOB TRADITION

Toward the end of the collection of oracles in their present arrangement, Hosea used the behavior of the patriarch Jacob as a metaphorical comparison of the contemporary leaders of Israel.

> Ephraim has encompassed me with lies,
>   and the house of Israel with deceit. . . .
> The Lord has an indictment against Judah,
>   and will punish Jacob according to his deeds.
> In the womb he took his brother by the heel,
>   and in his manhood he strove with God.
> A trader, in whose hands are false balances,
>   he loves to oppress.
> Ephraim has said, "Ah, but I am rich,
>   I have gained wealth for myself."
> (Jacob fled to the land of Aram,
>   there Israel did service for a wife,
>   and for a wife he herded sheep.)
>
> (11:12; 12:1–3,7–8,12)

Hosea's interpretation of the Jacob tradition is entirely negative. Either Hosea was reinterpreting the tradition, or he was familiar with an earlier version of the tradition than the one which we are familiar with in the canonical book of Genesis. In Genesis Jacob is presented as a deceiver, but one who seeks God's blessing. He seems to come off as a lovable rascal. He is the nation's ancestor, but admirable for several reasons. First of all, the brother whom he cheats turns out to be the father of the Edomites. Since Genesis reached its final form as a Judaic product, anything which humiliated Edom was favored (see the book of Obadiah). The second element in the Genesis tradition has to do with Jacob in Aram. Lawrence Boadt in *Reading the Old Testament* says:

> The tricks and deceits of Jacob and Laban against one another gave delight to Israelite audiences who saw in this single combat between heroes a mirror of the battle between the nation Israel and the Arameans in later days (1 Kgs 20 and 22), in which Israel outfoxed Aram.[2]

The Jacob tradition which Hosea refers to holds no delight, however. Gale Yee writes:

> In Jacob, he creates a parallel between his contemporaries and the deceitful actions of their patronymic ancestor, Jacob/Israel. He traces Ephraim's business frauds and desire for wealth (12:7–8) back to Jacob who cheated his brother and strove with God. . . . He identifies Ephraim's present-day flight to foreign powers with Jacob's flight to a foreign land. In this foreign country, he is lowered to the status of a slave to obtain Rachel, who for Hosea will characterize the moral corruption of the North.[3]

THE CONCLUSION OF THE EIGHTH CENTURY ORACLES

The oracles of Hosea ben Beeri end on a somber note. Like Amos, he did not deliver his oracles of judgment against the rulers of Ephraim expecting them to change their ways. Repentance and the concept of returning to Yahweh was not an eighth century theological understanding. He sadly ended his oracles with a horrible description of the atrocities of Assyrian invasion inflicted on the innocent of Samaria. His oracles end with these excruciatingly graphic words:

> Samaria shall bear her guilt,
>> because she has rebelled against her God;
> they shall fall by the sword,
>> their little ones shall be dashed in pieces,
>> and their pregnant women ripped open (13:16).

We should remember that by mentioning the fate of the children, Hosea was declaring in vivid terms that because of the decisions made by the leaders of Israel to abandon Yahweh they were causing the destruction of their own future.

TEN FACTS CONCERNING THE ORACLES OF HOSEA BEN BEERI

In Chapter V where we discussed the development of the prelude to the book of Hosea (chapters 1–3) we listed six facts about the oracles of Hosea ben Beeri. We are now in a position to expand this list to ten items:

(1) The name of Hosea does not appear in his oracles. This is true of all oracles of eighth century prophets. When the name of the prophet appears, it is the later addition of an editor.

(2) Yahweh is sometimes the speaker and Hosea is sometimes the speaker. It is difficult to tell in some instances.

(3) Who are the addressees? The first oracle may be addressed to Hosea. From chapter 4 on, all oracles are addressed to the rulers of Israel in Samaria.

(4) Who is the mother? The mother can be the nation Israel, or the capital city of Samaria, where decisions are made. Yee says that Rachel, the mother of Joseph and Benjamin, is the mother. She bases this partly on the closing oracles of Hosea where Jacob is identified as the father. Rachel was Jacob's favorite wife.

(5) There is nothing specifically in the oracles of Hosea about idols. In this book we are contending that references to idols are later additions, some easily identified as exilic. In another of our books (*Prophet of Justice*) we maintained that Amos,

another eighth century prophet, never referred to idols in his oracles.[4] Idolatry was not an issue with these eighth century prophets. We will say more about this later.

(6) Hosea's favorite name for his nation is Ephraim. After the middle of the eighth century the Assyrians marched west to ravage the land of Israel, leaving only Samaria and the tribal hill country of Ephraim. It may be at this time that Hosea adopted the name Ephraim for what was left of Israel.

(7) The language of the oracles is picturesque with a frequent use of metaphor.

(8) There is nothing about Gomer in these oracles. She is not the mother. As a matter of fact she is not part of the oracles at all.

(9) There is nothing specifically in the oracles of Hosea about Baalism. This is the most difficult fact about the original oracles of Hosea with which we will have to deal. There are several reasons why this may come as a surprise to us.

(a) There are many references in the book of Hosea to the practices of Baalism. Without an understanding of the redactional history of the book in mind, the reader would assume that Hosea himself was preoccupied with the Israelites participating in the practices of the fertility cult. These objections were introduced into the book of Hosea by the Josianic redactor.

(b) In a popular but possibly mistaken conception of Gomer's role in the book (Hosea never mentioned her name), she is identified by many as a sacred prostitute. I believe there is no good reason to make this assumption.

(c) We have been influenced by the Deuteronomistic History which is determined (for good reason in the days of Josiah) to eliminate all Baalistic ritual behavior in Judah. The Deuteronomic History viewpoint concerning Israel, the northern kingdom, is that Israel was destroyed because the people worshiped other gods, including Baal. The zealous Deuteronomistic reform movement of the late seventh century has shaped our view of life in Israel, and has projected its own values into the previous century in such a convincing way, that it is difficult for the average Bible reader to see things any differently. Further on we will discuss the Deuteronomic scribe (Josianic redactor) who introduced the oracles condemning Baal into the book of Hosea.

This is the most difficult fact about the original oracles of Hosea with which we will have to deal. For this reason we have devoted the next chapter to this subject.

(10) The sin of the mother is in having hired lovers. The hired lovers are Assyria and Egypt (7:11 and 8:9–10).

THE PROPHET OF LOVE

The name of this book, *Prophet of Love,* as you may have reasoned by now, does not refer to Hosea ben Beeri, the eighth century prophet. The prophet of love is a composite picture which fully emerges from the book of Hosea only when it reaches its canonical form. Several authors made profound and powerful contributions to the development of this symbolic prophet, including the collector, who first put into writing the eighth century oracles, the Josianic redactor, who wrote in the latter days of the seventh century, and, finally, the exilic redactor.

The eighth century prophet laid the foundation on which the most profound metaphor for God's love was built. Hosea spoke powerful words of grief and rage when the leaders of Ephraim abandoned Yahweh, Israel's ancient and loyal God. But Yahweh had not abandoned Israel.

Before we can turn to the subsequent growth of the book during the seventh and sixth centuries, there is a matter to which we must give our attention. In Chapter VII we will discuss the relationship of Yahwism and Baalism in the eighth century.

CHAPTER VII

The Relationship of Yahweh and Baalism in the Eighth Century

In this book we have stated that the oracles of Hosea ben Beeri (the eighth century portion of the book) do not contain any polemical, condemnatory references to Baalism or fertility cult activity by the inhabitants of Israel. Most scholars do not take this view. Hosea is presented in most commentaries as a spokesperson for Yahweh in condemning Baalistic practices in the northern kingdom a hundred years before the Judahite reforms of Josiah, that grand effort to eliminate "Canaanite" religious practices, an effort which has become known to us as the Deuteronomistic reform. (Perhaps we should remind ourselves that the circle of Jerusalemite priests who considered themselves the descendants of the Levites, and who championed these late seventh century reforms, never called themselves Deuteronomists.)

Because of this widespread misunderstanding of Hosea's concerns, it is necessary for us to take a look at what we know about the relationship of Yahweh and Baalism in the eighth century. The truth is that we have very little *hard* information about this subject. Our chief source of information is the Deuteronomistic History, which makes it clear that Yahweh is the only true God Israelites can serve. Joshua challenges the people at Shechem:

> ... choose this day whom you will serve, whether the gods your fathers served in the region beyond the River, or the gods of the Amorites in whose land you dwell; but as for me and my house, we will serve Yahweh (Jos 24:15).

Another significant passage is the account of the encounter of Elijah and the prophets of Baal on Mount Carmel. Neither of these passages, as important as they are, appear in the history of the chronicler (1 and 2 Chronicles).

The first edition of the Deuteronomistic History appeared in the reign of Josiah, *before his death,* and covered the history of Israel from Joshua to Josiah. Both Joshua and Josiah are presented as the ideal servant of Yahweh, and in many respects the two (Joshua and Josiah) mirror each other in their Yahwistic leadership characteristics. In a dissertation entitled *The Double Redaction of the Deuteronomistic History,* Richard Nelson points out many similarities between Joshua and Josiah, and states that the ancient, obscure figure of Joshua was artfully fleshed out to resemble the image which the Deuteronomist wished to project for King Josiah.[1] In other words, Joshua was created in the image of Josiah and not vice versa. Needless to say, the chief purpose of the Deuteronomist was to save Judah/Israel by nationalizing, standardizing, and uniting the people around the cult of Yahweh in Jerusalem, under the control of the levitical priesthood. Remember, in Deuteronomy the only priests mentioned are the Levites.

In the story of Elijah we should remember that the encounter was not with prophets of a local Baal (or Baals) but with foreign prophets of a foreign Baal imported from Tyre by Jezebel, a daughter of a Phoenician king.

Our understanding of the relationship of Yahweh to Baal rests upon our view of the origin of Israel. If we believe that a united Israel, with a long previous existence, entered Canaan, crossing the Jordan from the east and driving out and destroying all or most of the inhabitants of the land (the Canaanites or Amorites), then we may be able to visualize Yahweh demanding total allegiance to himself and himself alone, and demanding the elimination of local gods regardless of their function.

There are many problems with this view, however, and in this book we are taking the view that Israel emerged in the highlands in the middle of the thirteenth century as an agricultural federation of heterogeneous groups (mainly indigenous peoples), and that the first god of Israel was El.[2]

Yahweh was introduced to Israel when a group with a strong exodus tradition joined the federation and convinced others that

Yahweh, a champion and defender of the underdog, was the ideal god for a weak and marginal people. Yahweh could defend his people against superior forces (see Chapter III). The fury of which Yahweh was capable is reflected in many scriptural metaphors. Yahweh is a man of war (Ex 15:3), a roaring lion (Am 1:2), and, in Hosea, a bear robbed of her cubs:

> I will fall upon them like a bear robbed of her cubs,
>   I will tear open their breast.
> and there I will devour them like a lion
>   as a wild beast would rend them (13:8).

As time passed, Yahweh, an imminent God with more personality than the remote and impartial El, assumed some of the characteristics of El. Eventually, later in the history of the nation, the two would be completely merged in the theology of Israel.

Baalism, with its fertility rites, was for centuries the indigenous religion of the area where Israel emerged. In the Deuteronomistic History, information concerning Baalism is fragmentary and almost always polemical. For several reasons we know that Baalism with its fertility rites was commonplace in Israel and Judah during the eighth century. Archaeology supports this. In an article in *Biblical Archaeology* entitled "What Happened to the Cult Figurines?" by Ephraim Stern, the author reports on the discovery of thousands of female figurines used in fertility rites in Israel, Judah, Edom, Philistia, and Phoenicia.[3] He writes:

> . . . clay figurines have been found by the hundreds—even by the thousands—all over Palestine in earlier periods [earlier than the exile and post-exilic periods] . . . including sites in the heartland of ancient Israel: at Arad, Beer-Sheva, Lachish, Megiddo, Taanach, Hazor and Dan.[4]

The author goes on to say that before the exile "it is impossible to distinguish between Israelite areas and pagan areas on the basis of the presence or absence of cultic figurines."[5]

I believe that if we look carefully at scattered scriptural passages in the Deuteronomistic History we will reach the conclusion (supported by archaeology) that at least until the days of Josiah, Baalism was very much at home in Israel/Judah. Here are some scriptural references:

(a) Gideon had another name, Jerubbaal, "Baal contends" (Jgs 7:1).

(b) Saul had a son Eshbaal, and Jonathan had a son named Meribaal (1 Chr 8:33).

(c) Solomon rebuilt a city for defense purposes called Baalath (1 Kgs 9:18).

(d) A redacted passage in the book of Hosea suggests that in Israel's past Yahweh was called Baal. "And in that day, says Yahweh, you will call me 'my husband,' and no longer will you call me 'my Baal' " (Hos 2:16).

(e) Ahab "erected an altar for Baal in the house of Baal which he built in Samaria" (1 Kgs 16:32).

(f) An interesting speech is made by Rabshakeh, an Assyrian captain to a besieged Jerusalem in the days of Hezekiah: "But if you say to me, 'We rely on Yahweh our God,' is it not he [Yahweh] whose high places and altars Hezekiah has removed, saying to Judah and Jerusalem, 'You shall worship before this altar in Jerusalem'" (2 Kgs 18:22). In this passage the implication is that the high places were the high places of Yahweh. In other Deuteronomic passages the implied interpretation is that all high places are an abomination to Yahweh. However, Israel's patriarchs, including prophets and priests, regularly worshiped at high places with no censor. At Gibeon, called the "great high place," Solomon offered sacrifices (a thousand burnt offerings) and it was here that Yahweh granted Solomon the gift of wisdom.

(g) Baalistic worship was carried on in the temple at Jerusalem, not only in the days of Manasseh (2 Kgs 21:3–7), but also in the days of Josiah *up until the time the book of the law was discovered and read to Josiah* (2 Kgs 22).

The above paragraph is amazing if you read 2 Kings 22 carefully. The author is telling us that Josiah was concerned enough to have the temple repaired, but that he did not see anything wrong with the location of the altars for Baal in the temple

until the book of the law was read to him. It was only then that
Josiah

> . . . commanded Hilkiah the high priest . . . to bring out
> of the temple all the vessels made for Baal, for Asherah,
> and for the host of heaven. . . . And he broke down the
> houses of the male cult prostitutes which were in the
> house of the Lord, where the women wove hangings for
> the Asherah. And he defiled the high places where the
> priests had burned incense from Geba to Beer-sheba (2
> Kgs 23:4–8).

The further implication is that the book of the law which was
discovered in the temple was the book of the law which Joshua
has written at the conclusion of his life (Jos 24:26).

The question we must ask ourselves is this: If there was a
clear choice which confronted the Israelites from the days of
Joshua, would it have been possible for Yahweh and Baal to have
co-existed throughout the entire history of Israel so that even in
the early days of Josiah's reforms Baalism was practiced, not only
on the scattered high places, but also in the temple?

With this brief review I am suggesting that it was possible
that the cultic purity demanded by the Deuteronomistic movement of the late seventh century was a new and different emphasis and that perhaps there was not such a clear choice which had
to be made between Yahwism and Baalism in the eighth century.

CONCLUSION

There are two reasons why I feel that it was possible for
Hosea ben Beeri to ignore the practice of Baalism in his oracles.
First, as was discussed above, it was not the clear issue in eighth
century Israel as it later became in seventh century Judah. The
relationship between Baal, a god of fertility, and Yahweh, the
ancient and long-standing protector and savior of Israel, was not
clearly understood. After all, no one was in charge of pure theology. There was no council on orthodoxy or a hierarchy to determine true doctrine in Israel. There were many scattered sites with

diverse traditions. Jeroboam's attempt to establish a state religion with state sanctuaries at Bethel and Dan was only partially successful. There were dozens of other cultic centers, including Gilgal, Megiddo, Jezreel, Shiloh, and Shechem. And there were hundreds of green trees (Deut 12:2).

Second, and more relevant, is the subject of Hosea's audience. Hosea did not direct his oracles to the general population of Israel. He did not address a general audience or seek to correct a "general" problem. His oracles, like the oracles of Amos of Tekoa, were directed to a specific audience and addressed a specific problem. Like Amos, his audience consisted of the powerful decision makers of Samaria. It was their decision which would provoke Yahweh to anger and lead to the final destruction of Israel. In the eighth century there was not an understanding or perception that the fate of the nation depended on the behavior of individuals living in rural areas. The relationship between a nation and its god was a group relationship. Only a person or persons representing the nation would determine the relationship between an official god and the nation.

This is spelled out clearly for us in the following verse commenting on the final destruction of Jerusalem by the Babylonians:

> Surely this [complete destruction] came upon Judah at
> the command of Yahweh, to remove them out of his
> sight, for the sins of Manasseh (2 Kgs 24:3).

This editorial comment reveals to us a common interpretation of the times—that the fate of the nation was determined by the behavior of the official representative of the nation.[6] The nation was good if the king was good; the nation was evil if the king was evil.

One hundred years earlier Hosea was saying to the king of Israel that his decision to ignore and rebuff Yahweh in favor of dependence on Assyria (and other foreign powers) for deliverance was an offense to Yahweh amounting to rejection, and would lead to the nation's destruction. This was the core of his message. He was not dealing with or confronting the ritualistic behavior of the farmers of Ephraim.

CHAPTER VIII

The Josianic Edition
of the Book of Hosea

One hundred years after the tragic events of 722 B.C.E. an event took place in Jerusalem which would mark the beginning of a new era in religious history, an era which continues in full force until this day and shows no sign of abating. As we read 2 Kings 22, we are casually informed that while workmen commissioned by King Josiah were repairing the temple in Jerusalem, a priest by the name of Hilkiah "accidently" discovered the book of the law.

> And Hilkiah the high priest said to Shapan the secretary, "I have found the book of the law in the house of the Lord." . . . And Shapan the secretary came to the king, and reported to the king, "Your servants have emptied out the money that was found in the house, and have delivered it into the hand of the workmen who have the oversight of the house of the Lord." Then Shapan the secretary told the king, "Hilkiah the priest has given me a book" (2 Kgs 22:8–10).

The significance of this incident is rooted in the response of King Josiah to the contents of the book.

> And when the king heard the words of the book of the law he rent his clothes. . . . "Go inquire of the Lord for me, and for the people, and for all Judah, concerning the words of this book . . . for great is the wrath of the Lord that is kindled against us, because our fathers have

not obeyed the words of this book, to do according to all
that is written concerning us" (2 Kgs 22:11–13).

For the first time in the history of Israel Yahweh was com-
municating his will to Israel through the words of a book,
through scripture. In the past Yahweh had communicated in
many ways.

(1) With a voice of his own (Ex 3:4–7).
(2) Through divine messengers (angels).
(3) Through dreams (Gen 28:12).
(4) Through visions (Gen 15:1).
(5) Through human servants (prophets).

During the reign of Josiah the age of written revelation began and the Deuteronomistic historian informs us of this by de-
scribing the action and reaction of Josiah to the reading of the
scroll. The reading of Yahweh's written word was reserved for
kings and priests in this early stage, but notice the Deuteronomistic effort to broaden the audience by carefully chosen words
in the above quotation. Josiah says, "Inquire of the Lord for me,
and *for the people, and for all Judah."* This is very important for
our understanding of the seventh century edition of Hosea. The
original oracles of Hosea, like the original oracles of Amos, were
directed not to the wider audience of "the people" but to the
decision makers of Samaria. The basic change in the seventh
century edition of the eighth century prophets is the audience to
which the oracles are applied. The Deuteronomistic movement
in its concern for centrality and standardization of necessity addressed the people and demanded a positive response from the
people.

SCRIBAL ACTIVITY DURING THE REIGN OF JOSIAH

The book of the law discovered in the temple later became
the core of the book of Deuteronomy (chapters 12–26). The implication is that this was the same book which Joshua had written
when he met with the elders of the tribes of ancient Israel at
Shechem.

So Joshua made a covenant with the people that day, and made statutes and ordinances for them at Shechem. And Joshua wrote these words in the book of the law of God (Jos 24:26).

Another significant fact concerning the discovery of the book of the law is that the name of the priest who discovered the book had the same name as the father of Jeremiah.

. . . Jeremiah, the son of Hilkiah, of the priests of Anathoth in the land of Benjamin, to whom the word of the Lord came in the days of Josiah (Jer 1:1).

In a fascinating book by Richard Elliot Friedman entitled *Who Wrote the Bible?*[1] the author develops several intriguing hypotheses including one concerning the book of the law and the first edition of the Deuteronomistic History. Friedman's theory states that the book of the law came from the priests of Shiloh, levitical priests who were competitors with the priests of Bethel, who were aaronid priests. Jeremiah was a levitical priest of Shiloh, and Barach was his scribe. Together they wrote an introduction and conclusion (later to be expanded) for the book of the law which became the book of Deuteronomy, and together they contributed to the *first edition* of the Deuteronomistic History which made its appearance before the death of Josiah.

There is no doubt that during the reign of Josiah there was a great amount of Deuteronomistic scribal activity in Judah. This scribal activity produced new, expanded editions of four eighth century prophets: Amos, Hosea, Isaiah, and Micah. How did the late seventh century edition of Hosea differ from the earlier edition?

THE JOSIANIC EDITION OF HOSEA

The Josianic redactor of the book of Hosea amended the oracles of Hosea to reinterpret the sin of Israel. For Hosea the sin of Israel had been the rejection of an ancient dependent relationship with Yahweh for deliverance from enemies. This rejection was overtly expressed by the leaders of Israel in the making of foreign alliances with Egypt and/or Assyria, depending on the circumstances. Foreign powers were the hired lovers to which Hosea referred.

> . . . Ephraim has hired lovers. Though they hire allies among the nations, I will soon gather them up (8:9–10).

For the Josianic redactor, however, the sin of Israel was not political but cultic. The Hosean conception of sin was redefined. If you want to recognize the additions of the Josianic redactor to the oracles of Hosea you will look for references to altars (especially at Bethel) and references to keeping—or, more precisely, not keeping—the law of Yahweh. The concerns of the Josianic redactor are identical to the concerns of the author of the seventh century edition of the Deuteronomistic History. The Josianic redactor may have been the Deuteronomist himself if there was such an individual.

When the Deuteronomist wrote his history of Israel he idealized the ancient past. He pictured the elders of a united Israel entering into a "covenantal" relationship with Yahweh and receiving from Yahweh a collection of laws which the nation was bound to observe. These laws were in the "book of the law." The law was concerned with centralization and standardization of cultic practices. Worship at any altar except the one selected by Yahweh was considered unacceptable and sinful.

> . . . you shall seek the place which the Lord your God will choose out of all your tribes to put his name and make his habitation there. . . . Take heed that you do not offer your burnt offerings at every place that you see; but at the place which Yahweh will choose in one of your tribes, there you shall offer your burnt offerings, and there you shall do all that I am commanding you (Deut 12:5–14).

Here are some of the additions of the Josianic redactor to the oracles of Hosea. Notice the combination of covenant breaking, disregard for the law, and the act of worship at altars apart from the chosen one:

> And since you have forgotten the law of your God,
>   I also will forget your children (4:6).

> Enter not into Gilgal, nor go up to Bethaven (4:15).

> . . . and they shall be ashamed because of their altars (4:10).

> Because Ephraim has multiplied altars for sinning,
>   they have become to him altars for sinning.
> Were I to write for him my laws by ten thousands,
>   they would be regarded as a strange thing (8:11–12).

For the Josianic redactor Israel did not know Yahweh, nor did it know his laws.

THE SCOPE OF THE JOSIANIC REDACTOR

The book of Hosea inherited by the Josianic redactor in the late seventh century contained an introduction (consisting of a portion of our chapters 1 and 2) followed by a collection of the original oracles of Hosea. The scribe who had first collected and arranged the oracles of Hosea (the collector) had contributed some very important material to the introduction. It had been the collector who had introduced the symbolic names of the three children and the name of Hosea's wife, Gomer. It had also been the collector who had inserted the words

> . . . for she is not my wife,
> and I am not her husband (2:2)

into Hosea's first oracle which had started with the words, "Plead with your mother, plead." By doing this the collector had introduced the idea of a divorce into what would become the prelude to the book of Hosea.

After the prelude, which is discussed in Chapter V, the Josianic redactor continued his redaction with the first two verses of chapter 4:

Hear the word of the Lord, O people of Israel;
> for the Lord has a controversy with the inhabitants of
> the land (4:1).

The first thing we notice about this redaction is that *the audience has changed.* Whereas Hosea addressed the powerful elite of Samaria (like Amos), the Josianic redactor addressed the people at large.

There is no faithfulness or kindness,
> and no knowledge of God in the land;
there is swearing, lying, killing, stealing, and committing
> adultery;
> they break all bounds and murder follows murder (4:1–2).

The people have broken the commandments of God (Deut 5:6–21). Lack of obedience to the law is the opening issue. Knowledge of God is a Deuteronomistic phrase. While these words are directed to Israel, the Josianic redactor introduces Judah early in his editorials:

Though you play the harlot, O Israel,
> let not Judah become guilty (4:15).

Judah also shall stumble with them (5:5b).

For you also, O Judah, a harvest is appointed (6:11).

Picking up the metaphor of the harlot from Hosea's first oracle, the Josianic redactor defines what he means by the term "harlot." It now has nothing to do with foreign political alliances, relating instead to false cultic practices:

Enter not into Gilgal
> nor go up to Bethaven (4:15).

Ephraim is joined to idols (4:17).

. . . and they shall be ashamed because of their altars (4:19b).

Bethaven, meaning "house of trouble" or "house of iniquity," is identified by scholars as a derogatory name for Bethel.[2] We know that the altar at Bethel was a particular target of the Deuteronomists. This is so for three reasons. First, Bethel was only a relatively short journey from Jerusalem, near the northern border of Judah. Second, Bethel had an ancient history as a cultic shrine which gave it some real protection from Deuteronomic threats. Third, Bethel was under the control of a priesthood which was competing with the levitical priesthood of the Deuteronomists for the control of the cult of Yahweh in Judah during the reign of Josiah.[3]

Editorial redactions of the Josianic redactor continue to be scattered throughout the book of Hosea, all permeated with a concern for obedience to the law of Yahweh and cultic practices. The last editorial contribution of the Josianic redactor is identified by Gale Yee in Hosea 10.[4]

> The inhabitants of Samaria tremble
>   for the calf of Bethaven.
> Its people shall mourn for it,
>   and its idolatrous priests shall wail over it,
>   over its glory which has departed from it.
> Yea, the thing itself shall be carried to Assyria,
>   as tribute to the great king.
> Ephraim shall be put to shame,
>   and Israel shall be ashamed of his idol.
>
> Samaria's king shall perish,
>   like a chip on the face of the waters.
> The high places of Aven, the sin of Israel,
>   shall be destroyed.
> Thorn and thistle shall grow up
>   on their altars;
> and they shall say to the mountains, Cover us,
>   and to the hills, Fall upon us (15:5–8).

The inescapable aspect of Yahweh's punishment has a counterpart in Amos:

Though they hide themselves on the top of Carmel,
from there I will search out and take them (Am 9:3).

The torah of the Deuteronomist (the book of the law) does
not separate the importance of its religious laws from the importance of its secular laws. False cultic practices—for example,
worshiping at high places, or anyplace besides the place chosen
by Yahweh—were considered every bit as wrong as breaking the
moral commandments regulating human/social behavior. Both
cultic and ethical violations provoked Yahweh to anger and in-
vited Yahweh's punishment. Both were violations of the ancient
covenant between Yahweh and the people of Israel/Judah.

Set the trumpet to your lips,
    for a vulture is over the house of the Lord,
because they have broken my covenant,
    and transgressed my law (Hos 8:1).

There is a clarification of the nature of the methods of the
Deuteronomist(s) which we should make at this time. The Deuteronomists (the Josianic redactor was a member of their circle)
thought of themselves as champions of an ancient foundation
upon which the true religion of Yahweh was built. We like to say
of the Deuteronomists that in the late seventh century their purpose was to purify the cult of Yahweh by purging it of all Canaanite and Assyrian influences. Their understanding of Israel's
past, however, was either faulty or biased. In the Deuteronomistic History Israel is presented as consisting of twelve tribes, all
related, united before they entered the promised land, and deeply
devoted to their God Yahweh.

Whatever symbolic truth is presented in this story, historically it does not come close to the facts. When Israel first came
into existence its first inhabitants were Canaanites and its first
God was El. Throughout the development of Israel as an identifiable people Canaanite religious practices were common. The
three annual feasts mentioned in the book of the covenant (see
Ex 23:14–17) were Canaanite long before they were Israelite.

What is the point of our discussion? It is this: The Deuteronomists presented themselves as conservatives, preservers of ancient traditions. This was only partially true, however. The Deuteronomists in some very important ways were innovators, opening new trails for the progress of theological understanding. Saul M. Olyan in his book *Asherah and the Cult of Yahweh in Israel* writes, "The Deuteronomistic school are evidently the innovators, though in their polemic they claim that their position is traditional and ancient."[5]

With this in mind, we have noted above the editorial activity in the book of Hosea of the Josianic redactor and his concern for what the Deuteronomists considered purification of the cult of Yahweh. The actions necessary for purification of the cult are found at the beginning of the torah of Deuteronomy:

> You shall surely destroy all the places where the nations whom you shall dispossess served their gods, upon the high mountains and upon the hills and under every green tree; you shall tear down their altars, and dash in pieces their pillars, and burn their Asherim with fire; you shall hew down the graven images of their gods, and destroy their name out of that place (Deut 12:2–3).

Contrary to the projection of these laws into the ancient past, I am suggesting that many of these forbidden practices were acceptable in earlier times.

THE JOSIANIC PERCEPTION OF YAHWEH

The Josianic (seventh century) perception of Yahweh was not the same as that of the eighth century. Because there were multiple shrines in the eighth century where Yahweh was worshiped, under the control of competing priesthoods, it may not be possible for us to speak of a general or unified view of Yahweh in Israel or Judah in the eighth century. We can assume that the theology of Israel was not identical to the theology of Judah. We can also be sure that the perceptions of Yahweh in the rural areas of towns and villages were not the same as the perceptions of

Yahweh held by those who ruled capital walled cities such as Samaria and Jerusalem.

In the Josianic age we have an entirely different situation. Here was a grand effort to standardize the religion of Yahweh. The many written documents we have at our disposal from the Josianic age tell us clearly who Yahweh was and what kind of a god he was perceived to be at that time.

In the seventh century Yahweh was a god of laws. I use the plural word because there were many laws, and in addition there was more than one collection of law. Both the levitical priests, with a possible link to Shiloh, and the aaronid priests, with a link to Bethel, agreed that Yahweh was a god of statutes and ordinances. It is easy to imagine Yahweh, in the late seventh century, expressing his will in statutes and ordinances, as a superior party in a structured covenantal relationship. I am suggesting however that Hosea ben Beeri did not perceive of Yahweh as a partner of a structured covenantal relationship. The word "covenant," *brith,* appears five times in the book of Hosea. Only one time does it appear in the original oracles of Hosea, and then the parties are identified as Ephraim and Assyria (12:2b). The Yahweh of Hosea was not an aloof god of laws, but a dynamic champion of his people, the leaders of whom had turned their back on him.

SUMMARY OF THE JOSIANIC REDACTION

Here is a list of the redactional characteristics of the Josianic redactor:

(a) The Josianic redactor redefines the sin of Israel. The harlotry involved cultic activity rather than political decisions.

(b) The audience is enlarged to include the masses. "For Yahweh has a controversy with the inhabitants of the land" (4:1).

(c) Worshiping at high places or any place other than the place chosen by Yahweh is condemned.

(d) Bethel is particularly singled out for attack and is called Bethaven (house of iniquity).

(e) Yahweh is a distant god preoccupied with statutes and ordinances.

(f) The Josianic redactor concludes his redaction by explaining the fall of Israel as punishment for the sin of Jeroboam, the erection and the support of the calves of Dan and Bethel, especially Bethel:

> The inhabitants of Samaria tremble
>   for the calf of Bethaven.
> Its people shall mourn for it,
>   and its idolatrous priests shall wail over it,
>   over its glory which has departed from it.
> Yea, the thing itself shall be carried to Assyria,
>   as tribute to the great king.
> Ephraim shall be put to shame,
>   and Israel shall be ashamed of his idol (10:5–6).

As it turned out, the reforms of the Deuteronomistic movement were what the cult of Yahweh needed to move it away from being just another Canaanite cult and move it in the direction of becoming a religious movement of unmeasurable influence and power in the subsequent history of western civilization. These Deuteronomistic reforms, however, were not accomplished in the seventh century. With the untimely death of King Josiah the Deuteronomistic reforms came to a crashing halt. As we read the closing chapters of 2 Kings following the death of Josiah, we learn that the kings who followed him did not support the Deuteronomistic reforms. Very quickly Judah became a vassal of Egypt, and within forty years the capital city of Jerusalem was completely destroyed along with the temple. The inhabitants of Jerusalem were carried away into Babylonian captivity, although some remained behind in rural areas, and some fled to Egypt.

Fortunately many scrolls containing important religious writings of Israel were preserved by the Judahites, including the seventh century edition of the book of Hosea. Fifty years after the tragic events of 597, this book would grow and change once again as the result of the activity of an exilic redactor who would bring it to its canonical form.

CHAPTER IX

The Final Author

> And in the thirty-seventh year of the exile of Jehoiachin
> king of Judah, in the twelfth month, on the twenty-
> seventh day of the month, Evil-merodach king of Baby-
> lon, in the year that he began to reign, graciously freed
> Jehoiachin king of Judah from prison; and he spoke
> kindly to him, and gave him a seat above the seats of the
> kings who were with him in Babylon (2 Kgs 25:27–28).

The above verse is one of the closing verses of the Deuteronomistic History (Joshua, Judges, Samuel, Kings). It is usually
perceived as a perfect illustration of the meaning of the word
"anticlimatic." The incident seems strikingly unimportant considering all that went before. Besides, who cares about what happened to Jehoiachin in the thirty-seventh year of his captivity? It
seems irrelevant, but it is not. On the contrary this verse is very
important.

After the death of Josiah, the Deuteronomistic History
limps to a sad ending. King Jehoiachin appears to have surren-
dered to the king of Babylon without a fight in 597 B.C.E:

> . . . and Jehoiachin the king of Judah gave himself up to
> the king of Babylon, himself, and his mother, and his
> servants, and his princes, and his palace officials. The
> king of Babylon took him prisoner in the eighth year of
> his reign, and carried off all the treasures of the house of
> the Lord, and the treasures of the king's house, and cut
> in pieces all the vessels of gold in the temple of the Lord
> (2 Kgs 24:12–13).

With all the important and monumental things which happened to Judah from the days of Josiah on, Jehoiachin appears to

103

us as an uninteresting and insignificant character. Why then is the report of the changed status of Jehoiachin in the thirty-seventh year of his captivity important?

It is important for two reasons: (a) It may come as a surprise, but the Bible gives us no account whatsoever of the plight of the Judahites in captivity apart from this statement about Jehoiachin. It is the only straightforward narrative statement that we have about the events of the captivity period before the edict of Cyrus (538) which officially ended the forced captivity of the Judahites. (b) Even though this incident seems insignificant, it reveals something extremely important to us. It informs us that a vital change occurred in the relationship of the captive community and the Babylonian overlords. It does not serve our purposes in this book to speculate concerning what political changes took place to bring about the release of Johoiachin from prison.

But it is our concern to note theological changes which took place in the captive community as the years moved on. We may assume that the key word to describe the theology of the early exiles was despair. Yahweh had not saved Judah or Jerusalem. Why not? Was he weaker than the gods of the Babylonians? Had he lost interest in Judah and deserted it? Was the destruction of Judah punishment from Yahweh, and if so was there no hope for the future?

Deprived of the city of Jerusalem and the temple, the only thing the exilic community was able to take with it was the writings. These writings included, but were not limited to, the first edition of the Deuteronomistic History and the seventh century editions of prophets such as Amos, Isaiah and Hosea. These writings grew in importance as decades passed. The central place of "holy" scriptures in the religion of Israel started to be taken for granted. Copies of the law (torah) and some prophetic books were read, studied, memorized and adored.

Later in the exilic period, sometime after 561, the year that Jehoiachin was released from prison, a strong, optimistic faith began to replace the despair of the early years. The priests, prophets, and scribes of the Judahites were able to provide answers to the questions of the people. One of these answers appears in the exilic update of the Deuteronomistic History by an unknown person (or persons) who was an heir of the seventh century Deuteronomists. He added speeches to the first edition of the Deuteronomistic History, inserting them in key places in the history and attributing them to important persons. One of these speeches was attributed to Solomon and appears as a dedicatory prayer for the temple. Notice how appropriate these words are for the exilic community:

> If they sin against thee . . . so that they are carried away captive to the land of the enemy, far off or near, yet if they lay it to heart in the land to which they have been carried captive, and repent, and make supplication to thee in the land of their captors, saying, "We have sinned . . . then hear thou in heaven thy dwelling place their prayer and their supplication, and maintain their cause and forgive thy people who have sinned against thee, and all their transgressions which they have committed against thee; and grant them compassion in the sight of those who carried them captive, that they may have compassion on them (1 Kgs 8:46–50).

Not only was the Deuteronomistic History updated. The books of the prophets were also updated by the same circle involved in the updating of the Deuteronomistic History. We turn now to the details of the sixth century edition of the book of Hosea.

THE EDITION OF HOSEA INHERITED BY THE EXILIC REDACTOR

We remind ourselves that the book of Hosea inherited by the exilic redactor was not simply a collection of eighth century oracles. There had been two basic changes. First, the audience had been changed. Whereas the original oracles had addressed the king of Israel and his advisors, the Josianic edition had addressed a general audience of the people of Judah. Second, the sin of Israel had been updated. Originally the sin was trusting in foreign alliances instead of Yahweh for deliverance. In the Josianic edition the sin was participation in the "Canaanite" religious practices which were directed to the Baals to ensure fertility.

BRACKETING BY THE EXILIC REDACTOR

The first thing we notice about the work of the exilic redactor of the book of Hosea was his practice of bracketing.[1] He brackets the entire book by supplying the opening and closing verses for what would become the canonical book, and also provides paragraphs to separate the recognized sections of the book. His opening verse is:

> The word of the Lord that came to Hosea the son of Beeri, in the days of Uzziah, Jotham, Ahaz, and Hezekiah, kings of Judah, and in the days of Jeroboam the son of Joash, king of Israel (1:1).

While this verse seeks to anchor the activity of Hosea in the history of the nation, betraying a Judean bias by mentioning the Judean kings first, the closing verse is theologically more interesting:

> Whoever is wise, let him understand these things;
>   whoever is discerning, let him know them;
> For the ways of the Lord are right,
>   and the upright walk in them,
>   but transgressors stumble in them (14:9).

This verse is immediately identified by form as belonging to the category of ancient writing called wisdom literature. Wisdom literature in its secular characteristics was shared by many of the neighbors of Israel. Even in the Bible, wisdom is presented as an end in itself (wise for its own sake), and there frequently is no need for reference to Yahweh to enjoy its benefits. It may have been one of the developments of the exilic period that wisdom literature became more closely tied to the cult of Yahweh. In another study we noted how forms of wisdom literature were woven into the oracles of the prophet Amos (*Prophet of Justice*),[2] although Amos himself did not employ wisdom literary forms in his own oracles.

In providing the framework for the three sections of the book, what better theme could the exilic redactor select than the theme of returning? This would be music to the ears of the exiles. He ends each section with the Israelites returning.

> Afterward the children of Israel shall return
> and seek the Lord their God,
> and David their king (3:5).

> They shall come trembling like birds from Egypt,
> and like doves from the land of Assyria;
> and I will return them to their homes, says the Lord (11:11).

> They shall return and dwell beneath my shadow,
> they shall flourish as a garden (14:7).

In the above three verses we have identified the theme of "returning" in the material added by the exilic redactor. He actually used more material to separate the three sections of the book. He provided all five verses of chapter 3 to separate the allegory of the husband and wife in section I from the rest of the book. He provided all of chapter 11 to end section II, and all of chapter 14 (except verse 1 in English) to close the book. This is a good thing to know; if you want to isolate some exilic redactor material you can read chapters 3, 11, and 14.

If you do this you will note the key theme of the exilic redactor, the repeated theme of returning. Sometimes the return is to Yahweh:

> Take with you words, and return to Yahweh (14:2).

And other times the return is a journey back to Judah:

> . . . they shall come trembling like birds from Egypt,
> and like doves from the land of Assyria;
> And I will return them to their homes,
> says the Lord (11:11).

REPENTANCE AND RETURN

It may be difficult to understand the fact that the eighth century prophets did not deliver their oracles expecting a response from their hearers. One of the main reasons for this is that the canonical books of Amos and Hosea contain strong statements concerning an expected response from those who hear or read. The audience is encouraged and urged to respond:

Come, let us return to the Lord (Hos 6:1).

Sow for yourselves righteousness . . . for it is time to seek the Lord (Hos 10:12).

So you, by the help of your God, return, hold fast to love and justice, and wait continually for your God (Hos 12:6).

Take with you words and return to Yahweh, say to him, "Take away all iniquity; accept that which is good and we will render the fruit of our lips" (Hos 14:2).

It is our contention that all passages in the book of Hosea which encourage or exhort the audience to respond and repent are the editorial additions of the exilic redactor. Making the safe assumption that most of the exiles wanted nothing more than an opportunity to return to Judah, we note that our exilic redactor ties together the themes of returning to Judah and returning to Yahweh with the theological concept of repentance. The exilic redactor was introducing into the book of Hosea a profound theological development of the late exilic experience. Returning to Yahweh (repentance) and returning to the land were bound together. The physical, geographical return of the people of Yahweh was tied to the spiritual journey back to Yahweh. It may be that, during the exilic period, repentance, a religious doctrine which we now take for granted, became a central belief in Israelite religion for the first time, and that all references to repentance (confessing sin, being sorry for sin, and turning back to God) were projected back into the earlier religious history of Israel and back into the interpretation of Israel's ancient historical past. In support of this idea is the fact that in Deuteronomy (which reached its canonical form earlier than Leviticus) there is no mention of Yom Kippur, the day of atonement, as a national holiday for Yahweh's people.

It is with an allusion to repentance that the exilic redactor brightened the critical picture of Jacob which Hosea ben Beeri had presented. Hosea had painted Jacob as a deceiver who was the prototype of Israel's eighth century leaders who were filled with deceit. The exilic redactor uses a repentant Jacob to redeem the patriarch:

> He [Jacob] strove with the angel and prevailed,
>   he wept and sought his favor.
> He met God at Bethel,
>   and there God spoke with him. . . .
> So you, by the help of God, return
>   hold fast to love and justice,
>   and wait continually for your God (12:4–6).

The exilic redactor could do something which the Josianic redactor could not do. He could mention Bethel as the place of Jacob's blessing. It is the mention of Bethel which reveals to us that this passage is exilic. Although the exilic redactor was an heir of the Deuteronomists, the shrine at Bethel was no longer an issue as it had been in the days of Josiah. The Deuteronomistic History tells us that Bethel had been destroyed by Josiah and defiled forever. At any rate, during the exile, with Jerusalem in complete ruins, the competitive location of Bethel was just not an issue. The people of Israel and its theologians had more important issues to be concerned with.

A NEW EXODUS

The exilic redactor of the book of Hosea was a scribe, but he was much more than simply a person dedicated to the business of writing. He was a theologian.

Theological concepts are functional, and as such they come into existence and flourish only insofar as they meet the needs of an identifiable community. The exilic redactor engaged in an activity with which every preacher and teacher of religion is familiar. He referenced an older tradition and updated it by appropriating its truth to address a problem facing his contemporaries. The problem which his community faced was obviously the condition of bondage and captivity. Reduced to a minimum, the captivity community of displaced Judahites had this question: Is there hope for us?

The appropriate ancient tradition revised and updated by the exilic redactor and at least two other theologians of the exilic period was the exodus. Historically the exodus experience, literally reported as deliverance of twelve united tribes from Egyptian bondage by Yahweh's actions, involved only a few of the tribes which later came to make up the political body called Israel. In monarchical Israel, it is possible that the exodus tradition was valued more in the northern kingdom of Israel than in the southern kingdom of Judah. Regardless, in the late exilic period the exodus became the foundational symbol for all of the captives who found in it the basis for hope of deliverance for a weakened people who were willing to trust once again in their ancient god.

The exilic redactor was the first theologian to use the exodus experience for the center of his redactional activity. The second was the powerful, unknown poet whom we call deutero-Isaiah. The third person (or group) to update the exodus event was the aaronid priest who built the canonical book of Exodus around the earlier version which had consisted of the blended traditions of both J (the Yahwist) and E (the Eloist).

To set the stage for an exodus, the exilic redactor introduced into the allegory of the unfaithful wife (chapters 1–3) the concept of the hedging in of the stubborn, unfaithful wife.

> Therefore I will hedge up her way with thorns;
>   and I will build a wall against her,
>   so that she cannot find her paths (2:6).

The exilic redactor attached the above words to the words of Hosea ben Beeri:

For she said, "I will go after my lovers,
who give me my bread and my water,
my wool and my flax, my oil and my drink (2:5b).

In a few broad strokes the exilic redactor explained why Israel (Judah) went into captivity. She was unfaithful and stubborn and did not know what was in her own best interest. He also explained what Yahweh was going to accomplish with captivity: the obstruction placed between the wife and her ill chosen lovers would isolate her from them. In this "captivity" Israel would come to her senses. She would repent, turning back to her husband.

Then she shall say, "I will go and return to my first husband,
for it was better with me then than now (2:7).

Captivity was explained as the will of Yahweh for Israel's ultimate good.

Living in Egypt (and Assyria) became symbols for the Babylonian captivity.

They shall not remain in the land of the Lord;
but Ephraim shall return to Egypt,
and they shall eat unclean food in Assyria (9:3).

And also, building on the metaphor of the parent-child relationship, the exilic redactor writes:

When Israel was a child, I loved him,
and out of Egypt I called my son (11:1).

This clear reference to the exodus is used to introduce a further explanation of the captivity, using the symbolic names Egypt and Assyria for Babylon:

They shall return to the land of Egypt,
and Assyria shall be their king,
because they have refused to return to me (11:5).

But it was not the purpose of the exilic redactor merely to explain the cause and reason for the captivity. His greater pur-

TIME OF AUTHORSHIP	AUTHOR	SIN OF ISRAEL	WHAT IS REQUIRED OF ISRAEL?	NATURE OF YAHWEH
Latter part of the eighth century	Hosea and Collector	Making foreign alliances instead of trusting in Yahweh, Israel's savior of old	It is not clear—perhaps the initiative belongs entirely to Yahweh	A dynamic warrior who always defended Israel because of a long-standing relationship with Israel
Reign of King Josiah Latter part of the seventh century	A scribe of Jerusalem, a member of the deuteronomic circle	Participating in pagan religious rites, Assyrian and Canaanite Worshiping at the high places Not keeping the Torah of Yahweh Breaking the covenant	Destroy the high places, cease from Assyrian and Canaanite religious rites Worship only in Jerusalem Keep the Torah of Yahweh	Yahweh is a lofty God whose name dwells in the Jerusalem temple His relationship with Israel in the past is now thought of in the form of a highly structured covenant Above all Yahweh wants compliance with his statutes and ordinances
Late in exilic period Latter part of the sixth century	An heir of the former deuteronomic circle of Jerusalem	Not keeping the Torah Breaking the covenant Worshiping idols and false gods	Turn, return to Yahweh Repent Keep the Torah	Yahweh is lofty but is merciful Yahweh created and controls nature A universal God, nevertheless he remembers Israel

pose was to induce a healing, triumphant faith in the captive community. To do this the exilic redactor pictured Israel's future in terms of a journey. As we have already stated, the exilic redactor concluded all three sections of the canonical book with a journey back home.

> . . . and his sons shall come . . .
>> trembling from the west;
> they shall come eagerly like birds from Egypt
>> and like doves from the land of Assyria;
> I will return them to their homes,
>> says the Lord (11:10a–11).

All features of the exilic redactor's theology can be thought of as an exodus or a journey. There is movement from political slavery to freedom in Israel's own land. This was the socio-political reality upon which the grand theological concepts of Israel in the late exilic period were built. The sociological approach to Bible study has made it unnecessary for us to separate the sacred from the secular. At each step of Israel's development, an understanding of the socio-political status of the Old Testament people assists us in comprehending the people's needs and the relationship of theological developments.

A God who could control history, as Yahweh was now perceived as doing, in a purposeful captivity of his people by the manipulation of world powers (Babylon, Persia), was certainly a God worthy of Israel's faith. The ultimate purpose was to prepare Israel to receive Yahweh's love. It was the exilic redactor who reversed the negative names of the three symbolic children of Hosea:

> . . . and in the place where it was said to them,
>> "You are not my people,"
> it shall be said to them,
>> "Sons of the living God" (1:10).

The chief metaphor for the exilic redactor was a "journey" theme, a journey from barrenness to fertility (2:15; 14:7), from despair to hope, from captivity to home and freedom (11:11), from sickness to health:

> Come, let us return to Yahweh;
>   for he has torn that he may heal us;
>   he has stricken, and he will bind us up.
> After two days he will revive us;
>   on the third day he will raise us up,
>   that we may live before him (6:1–2).

All of these journey themes can be summed up as a journey from alienation to a new loving intimacy with Israel's God. And this brings us to the final chapter of this study.

CHAPTER X

Spiritual Lessons from the Book of Hosea

Oh the depth of the riches and wisdom and knowledge
of God! How unsearchable are his judgments and how
inscrutable his ways (Rom 11:33).

In this book we have told a straightforward story of the development of the book of Hosea over a two hundred year period.
Unfortunately life never moves in a straightforward way; there
are frequent regressions with circular and lateral movements. It is
only fair to remind ourselves that in our effort to sort out the
various layers of authorship in the book of Hosea we have over-
simplified some serious developments in the book's history. Nevertheless I believe that dealing in greater detail with our subject
would be counter-productive for at least some of us. However we
are already in a position to answer the important question concerning the spiritual meaning of our findings.

We will proceed in this chapter in a methodical way. For
each of the authors/editors we will ask the questions: (1) What
did the author mean by the name Israel? (2) What was the author's understanding of Yahweh?

HOSEA BEN BEERI

Hosea was a passionate champion of Yahweh. Although we
can only attribute to him a portion of the oracles of the canonical
book, it is his oracles which provide the foundation of the book.
When Hosea speaks of Israel he is speaking of a political entity at
a time of chaos, instability, and decline. In the twelve year period

following the death of Jeroboam II three of the four kings acquired the throne by murdering their predecessor. The political survival of this turbulent nation was threatened from the east by Assyria and from the west by Egypt.

Hosea's hope for Israel's future, based upon inherited values, was destroyed by the vicious and foolish decisions of Samaria's rulers in their willful determination to abandon Yahweh in favor of alliances of intrigue with the two military powers which threatened its existence.

We notice that Hosea often calls Israel Ephraim. In 733 Tiglath-pileser destroyed Damascus and stripped from Israel the northern portion called Galilee and territory east of the Jordan River. It is possible that Hosea used the name Ephraim for the reduced state of Israel.

Based on ancient traditions, Hosea perceived of Yahweh as a warrior God who revealed himself to Israel as a capable defender and savior. When Israel was first formed, composed of weak tribes huddled together for mutual survival, a pact with Yahweh had been entered into. The relationship between Yahweh and Israel which Hosea championed did not in any way resemble the vassal treaty covenantal relationship of Josianic times.[1] It was more like a living relationship, a bond of friendship, than a legal contract. There is nothing in the oracles of Hosea to suggest a structured covenant, nor was Yahweh perceived of as a covenant-loving God.

We stated earlier that with the exception of the first oracle, Hosea's oracles were all addressed to the powerful elite of Samaria, the political leaders of the nation. To whom then is the first oracle addressed?

> Plead with your mother, plead—
>> that she put away her harlotry from her face,
>> and her adultery from between her breasts (2:2).

In the eighth century it was common for prophetic oracles to consist of language borrowed from the courts. The word translated "plead" is *rib*. It means to bring a suit against, or to bring charges against, in a court of law. Considering that Yahweh is the speaker (who can "make her like a wilderness, and set her like a parched land, and slay her with thirst"), I think it is possible that this first oracle may be a primitive prophetic call, a call to Hosea to be a prosecutor of the accused mother. Hosea answered this call by delivering his harsh oracles.

And this brings us to another subject. Hosea was fond of metaphor, and it is he who begins the tradition of multiple metaphors which characterizes the entire book at each stage of its development. If you look at the metaphors of Hosea, however (see our chart entitled, "Metaphors in Hosea for Israel/Ephraim by Author"), you will see that his are all negative. The comparisons are critical and there is no tenderness in them. Another thing to notice about Hosea's metaphors is that the harlot is a mother, but she is not a wife. It was not Hosea who introduced the metaphor of the husband and the wife for which the book is best known. Nor did Hosea mention the name of his wife Gomer. This would come later.

As a champion of Yahweh, Hosea was a prophet of faithfulness. His oracles are powerful and inspired and reveal him to be a true poet. Like works of great art which endure, his oracles are still powerful today, and as we read them it is difficult for us not to attribute to him the more fully developed theology of a later Israel. This is what we can learn from him. Before a substantial structure can be erected, someone has to lay a foundation. His oracles provided part of the foundation on which other inspired writers would build profound theological concepts, understandings which would serve the spiritual needs of a great portion of mankind for a thousand generations. Hosea was furious with the decision makers of Samaria. They had turned their backs on Yahweh, Israel's savior. Hosea was an advocate for the preservation of ancient values. His oracles remind us that there are times which require furiousness and conviction; there are times which demand them.

The value and legitimacy of Hosea's oracles were not lost on the levitical scribes of Jerusalem in the days of King Josiah when the nation and the cult of Yahweh were faced with a great opportunity. Before we turn to that opportunity we must look at the work of the collector.

METAPHORS IN HOSEA FOR ISRAEL/EPHRAIM BY AUTHOR

HOSEA

2:2	GUILTY MOTHER
2:4b	HARLOT
5:13	A SICK PERSON
7:8	A CAKE NOT TURNED
7:9	GRAY HAIRED MAN
7:11	A SILLY DOVE
8:8	A USELESS VESSEL
8:9	A WILD ASS
9:16	DRIED UP FRUIT TREE
10:11	TRAINED HEIFER
12:7a	DISHONEST MERCHANT
13:13	AN UNBORN SON

COLLECTOR

2:2ff.	WIFE
2:7a	HARLOT

JOSIANIC REDACTOR

4:16	A STUBBORN HEIFER
9:10	GRAPES IN THE WILDERNESS
9:10	FIRST FRUIT ON FIG TREE
10:1	A LUXURIANT VINE

EXILIC REDACTOR

7:16	A SLACK BOW
11:1	A CHILD, A SON
13:3	MORNING MIST OR DEW
13:3	CHAFF THAT SWIRLS
13:3	SMOKE FROM A WINDOW
13:5–8	A HERD IN DANGER
14:5	A LILY
14:5–6	A HEALTHY POPLAR TREE
14:7	A GARDEN, A VINE

THE COLLECTOR

Following the destruction of Samaria in 722 B.C.E., Israelites who were able fled in all directions. As you might suspect many surfaced in Jerusalem, the capital city of the sister nation of Judah. It was here during the reign of Hezekiah (715–686) that the first written edition of Hosea's oracles appeared. The introduction provided by the collector, whose hand is detected only in chapters 1 and 2, affected profoundly the way subsequent editors and readers would understand the book.[2] The collector introduced the names of the three symbolic children, Jezreel, Not Pitied, and Not My People. He also mentioned the name of Hosea's wife, Gomer.

By introducing the three children and Gomer, the collector forever changed the significance and identity of the mother against whom Hosea was to bring suit. The mother, who was originally Israel, Samaria, or Rachel (the eponymous ancestor of Ephraim), became Gomer.

Another important change took place at this point. The collector, looking back on the historical fact of Israel's destruction, added these words after the words "Plead with your mother, plead—"

. . . for she is not my wife
and I am not her husband (2:2b).

By adding these words the collector introduced the metaphor of a divorce. Hosea had said nothing about a husband. Also, he had said nothing about a wife.

With his introduction, the collector added another layer to the foundation which Hosea had laid. If eighth century prophets had disciples (about which we know little), then the collector can be called a disciple of Hosea. Like other great contributors to the scriptural heritage, the collector realized the importance of recording the inspired words of Hosea because time was passing by, and the future needed a written record of the oracles. It is because of him that we have a book called Hosea. He is one of the many unnamed scribes of the Hebrew Bible to whom we are indebted.

The world has grabbed firmly the implications which the collector made possible with his inference that Yahweh was an offended husband and Israel an unfaithful wife.

THE JOSIANIC REDACTOR

The first major update of the written collection of Hosea's oracles was the work of a Josianic scribe (640–609) whose work must be viewed in the context of the great Deuteronomistic reform program of centralization and standardization of the cult of Yahweh in Judah. It was he, the Josianic redactor, who redirected the oracles of Hosea from addressing the decision makers of Samaria to addressing the people as a whole.

> Hear the word of the Lord, O people of Israel;
> > for the Lord has a controversy with the inhabitants of the land (4:1–2).

And it was he who redefined the sin of harlotry from foreign alliances by Israel's leaders (8:9–10a) to participation of the people in what the Deuteronomists considered "Canaanite" or pagan religious practices unacceptable to Yahweh. Because the people were ignorant and did not "know" Yahweh, they thought that the fertility gods provided them with the produce of the land.

> And she (Israel) did not know
> > that it was I who gave her
> > the grain, the wine, and the oil (2:8).

For the Josianic redactor the name Israel meant the northern kingdom, a political and geographic entity which had been destroyed one hundred years earlier. The cultic behavior of the citizens of the northern kingdom, according to the Josianic redactor, led to the destruction of the nation. Israel, for the Josianic redactor, was an object lesson. His primary concern for his contemporary audience in Judah was the absolute necessity of cultic purity. This included worshiping at the place which Yahweh had chosen and refraining from participation in cultic practices which were forbidden by Yahweh and which were an abomination to him. In this light we can read these verses:

> Though you play the harlot, O Israel,
>   let not Judah become guilty.
> Enter not into Gilgal,
>   nor go up to Bethaven....
> Ephraim is joined to idols ...
>   and they shall be ashamed because of their altars
>   (4:15–19).

Ephraim has multiplied altars for sinning (8:11).

The Josianic redactor's perception of Yahweh was not that of an imminent God close at hand to deliver his faithful people. Yahweh is now an exalted, distant God. Only his name dwells in Jerusalem. This Yahweh is a God of law, and there is no trouble understanding him as a covenant-loving God. According to the Josianic redactor the northern kingdom was punished because the inhabitants didn't remain true to or understand the laws of Yahweh:

> Were I to write for him [Ephraim] my laws by ten
>   thousands,
>   they would be regarded as a strange thing (8:12).

The Josianic redactor was a member of the Deuteronomistic circle, and the Deuteronomists are sometimes criticized for being too legalistic. One common criticism of the Deuteronomists is that in their theology the rich, healthy, and victorious are the righteous as evidenced by God's blessing, and the poor, the weak, the marginal, the defeated, are the cursed of the earth (Deut 28:15–68) and have not received God's blessings because they have not honored God's laws. Whatever the merit of this argument, we must not underestimate the tremendous role which the Deuteronomists played in the development of Judah's religion. In their effort to standardize the practices of the cult of Yahweh they made all the right decisions. Their polemic against idolatry and other "abominable" practices in the name of religion, including child sacrifice and cult prostitution, raised the religion of Israel forever above an assortment of ancient pagan practices of Canaan and Assyria. They made all the right decisions, forbidding activities which debased the dignity of humans and insulted the majesty of God.

In addition to "cultic purity," this circle of Judaic levitical priests promoted a torah which placed heavy emphasis on ethical, social obligations. It was the Josianic redactor who added to the book of Hosea these words:

> Hear the word of the Lord, O people of Israel;
>> for the Lord has a controversy with the inhabitants of the land;
>> there is swearing, lying, killing, stealing, and committing adultery;
>> they break all bounds and murder follows murder (4:1–2).

The activity of the Deuteronomists itself contains a great spiritual lesson for us. After the tremendous output of the circle, including the first edition of the Deuteronomistic History, the book of Deuteronomy, and an updated version of four eighth century prophets, the movement came to a crashing halt with the sudden death of King Josiah. After the death of Josiah, life in Judah was all downhill, culminating in the destruction of Jerusalem and the temple by the invading Babylonians. Some Judahites fled to Egypt, and the leading citizens of Jerusalem were taken to foreign captivity. At this point the morale of the Deuteronomists was completely destroyed, and they had to believe that their efforts had been completely in vain, a waste of time, energy, and faith. There are times in life when the great victory won is not obvious until some time passes.

Today the whole world knows of the great contribution to the development of religion made by this small band of zealous priests and scribes. The contribution of this small circle in seventh century Jerusalem, a city which was weak politically, economically, and militarily, was going to be so large in the history of the religion of mankind that its value cannot be measured. The book of Deuteronomy is considered by some to be the world's most influential book.

God chose what is weak in the world to shame the strong (1 Cor 1:27).

But there was another stage approaching, another giant step in the direction of understanding the majesty of God and the corresponding dignity of humankind.

THE EXILIC REDACTOR, PROPHET OF LOVE

Something happened late in the exilic period which turned the despair of the captivity people into an optimism of healing faith. The exilic redactor played a role in this transformation. When the exilic redactor spoke of Israel he certainly was not speaking of the political entity called the northern kingdom which had ceased to exist after 722 B.C.E. For him the name Israel meant the people of Yahweh, a weakened people, a people in need of restoration. The metaphors which the exilic redactor uses for Israel contain nothing of the bitterness of Hosea but are all reflections of fragility or tenderness. (See our chart "Metaphors in Hosea for Israel/Ephraim by Author".) The exilic redactor used the ancient name Israel for Yahweh's people, now a captivity community, a community whose attention he addressed with repeated figures of a journey home.

Afterward the children of Israel shall return and seek the Lord their God, and David their king; and they shall come in fear to the Lord and to his goodness in latter days (3:5).

The exilic redactor's perception of Yahweh, which he shared with other late exilic prophets, including deutero-Isaiah, was of a majestic, all-powerful God who was also a God of mercy. A captive Israel primarily had need of spiritual healing and nurturing. At this time in its existence, the political and military needs of former centuries were completely irrelevant. The exilic redactor explains the meaning of captivity by *expanding* the metaphor of the husband and wife as it appeared in the edition of Hosea which he inherited.

The exilic redactor pictured Israel as the wife of Yahweh, who is a strong, wise and loving husband who will not allow his beloved to continue in her foolish, self-destructive behavior. So he constrains her, hedges her up, so that she cannot continue in her unwise pursuit of unworthy lovers:

> Therefore I will hedge up her way with thorns;
>   and I will build a wall against her,
>   so that she cannot find her paths (2:6).

After a period of constraint she will come to her senses and repent. Then her loving husband will be able to heal her and restore her to her former place.

> Then she shall say, I will go
>   and return to my first husband,
>   for it was better with me then than now (2:7b).

> Therefore, behold, I will allure her,
>   and bring her into the wilderness,
>   and speak tenderly to her.
> And there I will give her her vineyards,
>   and make the valley of Achor a door of hope.
> And there she shall answer me
>   as in the days of her youth (2:14–15).

Of the four authors of the book of Hosea, the exilic redactor is the one who has earned the title "Prophet of Love." His expansion of the text he inherited produced the final edition of the book and added a powerful theological dimension based on his lofty perception of Yahweh and on his insight into the relationship between Yahweh and his people Israel. It was he who reversed the negative meaning of the names of the three children of Hosea. When he received the metaphor of the marriage between Yahweh and Israel, the meaning of the metaphor was centered on the wife's infidelity. When he completed the metaphor the emphasis had shifted to the tenacious love of the wise husband.

Above we discussed the exilic redactor's theological explanation of the captivity. It was a necessary hedging and blocking of the unfaithful wife to bring her to her senses and prepare her for restoration. The necessary, expected result of Israel's response is explained by the exilic redactor:

> Come, let us return to the Lord;
> > for he has torn, that he may heal us;
> > he has stricken, and he will bind us up.
> After two days he will revive us;
> > on the third day he will raise us up,
> > that we may live before him (6:1–2).

Almost everything that the exilic redactor touched he brightened. Take for example the place of Jacob the patriarch in the exilic redactor's edition of the book. For Hosea ben Beeri Jacob was an example of a deceiver who symbolized the deceit and treachery of the Samarian elite during the eighth century. The exilic redactor changes this and makes the patriarch a hopeful symbol. First he adds the words:

> He strove with the angel and prevailed,
> > he wept and sought his favor (12:4).

Jacob is thus cited as one who repents. Because he repents he receives assurance that he will return:

> . . . God spoke to him—
> the Lord the God of hosts,
> > the Lord is his name:
> "So you, by the help of your God, return,
> > hold fast to love and justice,
> > and wait continually for your God" (12:4b–6).

Because the nature of Yahweh is to love and show mercy, he cannot deal with Israel solely on the basis of law. The exilic redactor explains this by using the metaphor of the parent-child relationship.

> When Israel was a child, I loved him,
>   and out of Egypt I called my son . . .
>   it was I who taught Ephraim to walk (11:1, 3a).

After introducing this metaphor the exilic redactor mentions the rebellion of Israel in spite of Yahweh's tender love. Yahweh says, "My people are bent on turning away from me" (11:7). In Deuteronomy there is a law which allows the parents of a rebellious son to bring the son to the elders for execution (Deut 21:18–21). As rebellious, disobedient children, should the captives interpret their predicament as the destruction of Israel? Did they have no hope? The exilic redactor makes clear that there is hope and that this hope is based on Yahweh's nature. Yahweh will not allow what the law permits.

> How can I give you up, O Ephraim!
>   How can I hand you over, O Israel! . . .
> My heart recoils within me,
>   my compassion grows warm and tender.
> I will not execute my fierce anger,
>   I will not destroy Ephraim;
> for I am God and not man,
>   the Holy One in your midst,
>   and I will not come to destroy (11:8–9).

According to law a rebellious son deserved punishment. In the development of Israel's theology law came before mercy; in the development of the book of Hosea, the Josianic redactor with his emphasis on law came before the exilic redactor, the prophet of love. Law comes before love, but God's love transcends law.

CODA

If I may employ one final metaphor, the book of Hosea is a mural to which several inspired artists contributed. This mural depicts the growth of Israel's understanding of its God, and, consequently, its relationship to God.

But since Hosea is a book, there are some important facts about the production of books in ancient Israel with which we should be familiar. In ancient Israel books were not written by individuals for the purpose of sharing the author's literary skills. Books were produced as the result of an ongoing community process which utilized the literary and scribal skills of several authors living at different times in completely different social and historical situations. Only a few short books of the Hebrew Bible were the products of individual writers.

There was a time in the development of redaction criticism when there was such delight in being able to identify the original oracles of the prophet for whom the book was named that there was a fear that too much value would be placed on them to the discredit of many later additions to the scroll. Recently the emphasis has completely shifted. In many recent scholarly books the practice is to emphasize the value and integrity of the finished product, the canonical book. We are reminded that it was the canonical book which the church pronounced as inspired. While there is truth here that cannot be denied, I do not believe that Bible students should ignore any step in the development of a prophetic book. Scholars will sometimes use weighted language to stress the unity of a book when it is obvious that the book is fragmented and contains contradictory statements. If we keep in mind that each author/editor was addressing a different set of problems and working in a different social environment, it will help us to appreciate the great value of the work of each contributor.

In the book of Hosea it was the exilic redactor who introduced the most powerful and profound theological insights and concepts. Nevertheless, he was not more inspired than the earlier contributors. Each author was inspired, and the entire book is the word of God.

We said in an earlier chapter that the prophet of love was a composite prophet who only emerged after the contribution of several authors. By this we mean that the exilic redactor built on the work of those who went before him. Hosea ben Beeri may not have been the prophet of love, but he surely was a prophet of faithfulness. He was zealous for Yahweh. The Josianic redactor added the necessity and importance of law, and emphasized that aspect of law which enhances human life, our obligations to each other. The religious practices condemned by the Josianic redactor were those which debased humanity and robbed humans of their dignity. Building on the foundations of these two prophets, the exilic redactor attributed his oracles to the eighth century prophet whose name was already recognized as belonging to one who championed the cause of Yahweh at a time when the strong and powerful had forgotten their ancient God.

The greatest spiritual lesson which our study of the book of Hosea teaches us is related to the emergence of the exilic redactor and his restorative theology. It is a fact that the most profound and most majestic perceptions of God, and God's relationship to Israel, came from a people who were completely without power, a captive people, with no wealth, no political influence, and no military strength. What better illustration could be found for the words of the apostle Paul?

God chose what is foolish in the world to shame the wise, God chose what was weak in the world to shame the strong, God chose what is low and despised in the world . . . so that no human being might boast in the presence of God (1 Cor 1:27–29).

Notes

PART ONE

I. THE HISTORICAL HOSEA

1. Walter Ferguson, *Journey Through the Bible* (New York: Harper and Brothers), 1945.
2. See R. H. Pfeiffer, *Introduction to the Old Testament* (New York: Harper and Brothers, 1948) p. 568.

II. WHAT WAS ISRAEL?

1. Norman Gottwald, *The Tribes of Yahweh* (Maryknoll: Orbis Books, 1979).
2. Ibid., Chapters 42 and 43, pp. 489–497.
3. David Hopkins, *The Highlands of Canaan: Agriculture in the Early Iron Age* (Sheffield: JSPT Press, 1985).
4. *The Tribes of Yahweh*, Chapter 49, pp. 608–621.

III. WHO WAS YAHWEH?

1. For example, see Martin Noth's book, *A History of Pentateuchal Traditions* (Chico: Scholars Press, 1981). An earlier edition was published in English by Prentice-Hall in 1972.
2. Richard Friedman, *The Exile and Biblical Narrative* (Chico: Scholars Press, 1981). In this book Friedman explains why it is evident that the first edition of the Deuteronomistic History appeared during the reign of King Josiah and not after his death.

V. THE ALLEGORY OF THE BAD MARRIAGE

1. See the commentary by H.W. Wolff, *Hosea, A Commentary,* trans. Waldemar Janzen et al. (Philadelphia: Fortress Press, 1974).
2. Dr. Gale Yee, in her book *Composition and Tradition,* fully referenced in our next note, reports that in a 1904 study K. Marti argues that chapter 2 should not be considered part of section I, chapters 1–3 (page 3).
3. Gale A. Yee, *Composition and Tradition in the Book of Hosea, A Redactional Critical Investigation* (New York: Scholars Press, 1987). This study deals comprehensively with the entire book of Hosea, illustrating in detail the scribal practices of the scribes of the seventh and sixth centuries, in particular the two we are calling the Josianic redactor and the exilic redactor. In Dr. Yee's book she calls them R1 and R2.

    In discussing the growth of the book of Hosea, Dr. Yee started with the final version of the book of Hosea, the canonical book, and worked her way back to the original eighth century oracles. She did this because she wanted to stress the value, the importance, and *the unity* of what she calls the final redacted state. In this chapter we are dealing with Hosea 1–3. Of this section Dr. Yee writes, "Exegesis of these chapters must reckon with the homogeneity as well as the heterogeneity within the story of Hosea's marriage" (p. 54).

    There is another reason for starting with the finished book and working backward. This has to do with the process of identifying the original oracles of Hosea *by elimination of oracles which can be attributed to others.* It happens that the oracles of the last redactor are the easiest to identify. This redactor, whom we call the exilic redactor, but whom Dr. Yee calls R2, used language which can be identified as exilic. Dr. Yee identifies his perceptions as being akin to DTR2. He was an heir of the seventh century Deuteronomistic circle.

    Dr. Yee wrote her dissertation, on which her published book is based, for a theological faculty, the members of which were all scholars, and were familiar with the canonical book. Starting with the "finished" book was very appropriate. In our book we move forward, however, starting with the original oracles, not because I believe this is a better way to approach the subject, but because I believe that it will be easier for the reader who may not be familiar with the final redacted state to follow the growth of the book of Hosea.

4. Ibid., pp. 112–115.
5. It is a popular and widespread belief that Hosea learned about Yahweh's feelings through his own painful marital experience. For example John Mauchline is quoted in the introduction to Hosea in *The Interpreter's Bible* (Nashville: Abingdon, 1956, p. 562), "The mystery of the compulsive power of his own love for Gomer made Hosea reflect upon the love of God for erring Israel." This is not what I am suggesting here at all. What I am saying is that the collector may have been the first author to reach that conclusion. However, from the evidence we have I do not believe that we can say with assurance that the historical Hosea had a bad marriage or a wife who did not return his love. As time went by he certainly had a *reputation* for having a harlot as a wife. H. Birkeland, a Norwegian, states in his book *Die Komposition der Prophetischen des Alten Testaments* (Oslo: Jacob Dybwad, 1938), that the wife of chapter 1 did not become a wife of harlotry until chapter 3 was added to the text at a later time.
6. Yee, *Composition and Tradition,* p. 115.
7. Ibid.
8. Read 2 Chronicles 34. Begin reading at verse 3 and continue reading through verse 16.

PART TWO

VI. THE ORACLES OF HOSEA

1. For an excellent, concise description of the vassal treaty structure, consult Lawrence Boadt's book, *Reading the Old Testament* (Mahwah: Paulist Press, 1984), pp. 173–182.
2. Ibid., p. 145.
3. Yee, *Composition and Tradition,* p. 306.
4. William J. Doorly, *Prophet of Justice* (Mahwah: Paulist Press, 1989).

VII. THE RELATIONSHIP OF YAHWEH AND BAALISM IN THE EIGHTH CENTURY

1. See Richard Nelson's book *The Double Redaction of the Deuteronomistic History* (Sheffield: JSOT Press, 1981), pp. 125ff.
2. This is one of the premises of *The Tribes of Yahweh,* previously cited.
3. *Biblical Archaeology* (July/August 1989, Vol. XV, No. 4), p. 25.
4. Ibid., p. 53.
5. Ibid.
6. Group identity was the rule in ancient Israel. In Micah 3:12 we are told, "Therefore because of you [the leaders, priests, and court prophets] Zion shall be plowed as a field." There are many other examples of group punishment because of the offenses of symbolic leaders. The largest group, mankind, was punished because of the sins of their first parents. Because of the sins of the fathers, God is said to visit his wrath to the third and fourth generation (Deut 5:9). In this case the group punished extends through time into the future.

VIII. THE JOSIANIC EDITION OF THE BOOK OF HOSEA

1. Richard Elliot Friedman, *Who Wrote the Bible?* (New York: Harper and Row), 1987.
2. Grace Emerson, in her dissertation entitled *Hosea, An Israelite Prophet in Judean Perspective,* suggests that the name Bethaven was a contemptuous name for the famous northern sanctuary (Sheffield: JSOT, 1984), p. 136.
3. Friedman, *Who Wrote the Bible?* p. 44.
4. Yee, *Composition and Tradition,* p. 296.
5. Saul Olyan, *Asherah and the Cult of Yahweh in Israel* (Atlanta: Scholars Press, 1988), p. 9.

IX. THE FINAL AUTHOR

1. Yee, *Composition and Tradition,* pp. 309–310.
2. William J. Doorly, *Prophet of Justice: Understanding the Book of Amos* (Mahwah: Paulist Press, 1989), pp. 52–55.

X. SPIRITUAL LESSONS FROM THE BOOK OF HOSEA

1. Brevard Childs in *Old Testament Theology in a Canonical Context* (Philadelphia: Fortress Press, 1985) writes: "Yet it is equally clear that the concept of covenant has been greatly expanded by the Deuteronomist and given a central role which it did not appear to have at first" (p. 93).
2. See Yee, *Composition and Tradition,* pages 307–308, and also the appendix beginning on p. 316.

Appendix

In Gale Yee's book *Composition and Tradition in the Book of Hosea,* which provides the basis for our divisions of the development of Hosea, she illustrates the editorial techniques of scribal redactors for every passage in the book of Hosea. Inherited oracles were appended and expanded in accordance with well-understood scribal practices which scholars refer to under the general heading of word play. The following technical terms are employed and illustrated in Yee's study.

Chiasm	Chiasm comes from the name of the Greek letter Chi (χ), because the bottom of the letter is a mirror image of the top. In a chiastic structure, the conclusion of the structure is a mirror image of the beginning. For example, the completion of chiastic structure for 123 would be 321.
Paronomasia	A comprehensive term referring to a variety of plays on words. In a limited sense it refers to a play on similar sounding words.
Metaphony	A form of paronomasia; the words added contain the same consonants as the section which is being amended.
Antanaclasis	The same words are used, or words with the same roots, but the meanings may vary. Dr. Yee notes a fivefold antanaclasis in Hosea 2:23–24 and in 14:2–8.

134

| Double Entendre | A group of words or an expression is used which lends itself to more than one meaning. |
| Alliteration | Words are used which repeat the initial consonants or syllables of neighboring words. |

Recommended Reading

The books in this section have been selected with the religious professional in mind. These are the persons who are so busy laboring in the world of human need that they simply may not have time to enjoy the luxury of digging into the vast amount of scholarship available. The field of Old Testament scholarship is currently complex, exciting, and expanding. Here are recommendations for the beginning and intermediate Bible student. We can assume that the advanced student has his or her own list of books and articles.

THE TOTAL PICTURE

You cannot understand a book of the Bible in a vacuum. For getting the broad picture, *Reading the Old Testament* by Lawrence Boadt (Mahwah: Paulist Press, 1984) gives an excellent picture of the entire Old Testament using a textbook approach with many helpful maps and charts. Two one-volume Bible commentaries which contain essential articles on O.T. history, customs, and concepts (along with commentaries for each book of the Bible, including Hosea) are *The Interpreters Bible* (Nashville: Abingdon, 1971) and *The Jerome Bible Commentary* (Prentice Hall, 1968). A new edition of the *Jerome Bible Commentary* was published in 1989.

THE BOOK OF HOSEA

The Scholars Press book by Gale Yee, *Composition and Tradition in the Book of Hosea, A Redactional Critical Investigation* (1987), is not a commentary. This study deals with the redactional development of the book of Hosea, illustrating in detail the linguistic/technical practices of the scribes of the seventh and sixth centuries, in particular, the two we are calling JR and ER. In Dr. Yee's book she calls them R1 and R2. This book should be read by every *serious* student of the Bible.

Conventional commentaries on the book of Hosea include *Hosea: A New Translation with Introduction and Commentary,* Anchor Bible 24 (Garden City: Doubleday and Company, 1980), by David Noel Freedman and Francis I. Anderson, and *Hosea, A Commentary,* translated by Waldemar Janzen et. al., Hermeneia Series (Philadelphia: Fortress Press, 1974) by Hans Walter Wolff. The commentary by James L. Mayes, *Hosea: A Commentary* (Philadelphia: Westminster, 1969), is a well written, conservative approach to the study of the book.

For an archaeological perspective, with many helpful insights into daily life of eighth-century Israel read *Amos, Hosea, Micah–An Archaeological Commentary* by Philip J. King (Philadelphia: Westminster, 1987).

For the intermediate student two books by J. Blenkinsopp are recommended; *Prophecy and Canon* (Notre Dame: University of Notre Dame Press, 1977) and *A History of Prophecy in Israel* (Philadelphia: Westminster, 1983).

OTHER RELATED SUBJECTS

Sections in the one-volume Bible commentaries mentioned above on the Deuteronomic school and the Deuteronomistic history should be read. Another slim volume on this subject is *Joshua, Judges, Samuel, Kings* by W.E. Rast (Philadelphia: Fortress Press, 1978).

For a short history of religion in ancient Israel consult *Israelite Religion* (Philadelphia: Fortress Press, 1966) by Helmer Ringgren.

For an excellent sociological approach to life in ancient Israel I recommend Part VI (pages 237–343) entitled "Models of the Social Structure: All Israel; Protective Associations; Extended Families," in *The Tribes of Yahweh* by Norman Gottwald (Maryknoll: Orbis Books, 1979). I also recommend David Hopkins' book *The Highlands of Canaan,* especially chapter IX, "Agricultural Objectives and Strategies: Risk Spreading and the Optimization of Labor," and chapter X, "Subsistence Challenges and the Emergence of Israel."

Finally, there are two fine books by Richard Elliot Friedman. For an exposition of the hypothesis concerning the existence of two competing torahs at the end of the seventh century consult *The Exile and Biblical Narrative* (Chico: Scholars Press, 1981). The other book is *Who Wrote the Bible* (New York: Harper and Row, 1987).